Loss & Redemption

Lessons from Naomi & Ruth

THOMAS OPPONG-FEBIRI

ISBN 978-1-0980-7301-5 (paperback)
ISBN 978-1-0980-7302-2 (digital)

Christian Faith Publishing, Inc.
832 Park Avenue
Meadville, PA 16335
www.christianfaithpublishing.com

All biblical quotations and the book of Ruth text are taken from the New Revised Standard Version Catholic Edition (NRSVCE).

www.lossandredemption.com
loss@redemption.com

Printed in the United States of America

In loving memories of my father Albert Kofi Febiri
and my sister Rebecca Adomah-Febiri

Contents

Acknowledgments

I am solely responsible for the content of this book, but I acknowledge that it is a fruit of encouragement, assistance, suggestions, and readings from others. To all of them, I remain forever grateful. A special thanks to Sidney Callahan, PhD. When I conceived of the idea of writing a book, Sidney was the first person I called and invited her to be a coauthor. She gladly accepted my invitation, but circumstances under COVID-19 restrictions couldn't realize our dream of cowriting a book. But she graciously followed with keen interest from the beginning to the end of the book and wrote the foreword. I was so delighted sitting down in her backyard going through the manuscript page by page on the Fourth of July, 2020, which happens to be my birthday. What a great birthday gift it was sitting at the feet of a great woman on Independence Day.

I am eternally grateful to Mary Lou Dillon because this book is an answer to her persistent question, "Thomas, when are you publishing the book?" Besides, she is my foremost editor to read through the manuscript with suggestions and corrections. I also thank Linda Trentacoste Spagnuolo, Esq., for encouraging me. I appreciate her and Joseph DiSalvo's, Esq., pro bono advice before signing the publishing contract.

With the help of three women, the book was drafted, and when it was ready for publishing, I reached out to three men to help me in the final stage of publication. I am indebted to three professors and authors—Jim Cullen, PhD, Tom Milton, PhD, and Rev. Michael K. Mensah, SSD—who graciously read the final draft and gave me a blurb. Thank you, three! I am especially grateful to Fr. Mike for reading the manuscript not with a biblical scholarship microscopic lens but with a pastoral perspective lens.

I thank my brother priest and friend, Rev. James Annor-Ohene, Esq., who drove me to Sidney's house to leave the first chapter of the manuscript in her mailbox and provided me serene hospitality to do the final editing. I am grateful to Rev. Joseph Domfeh-Boateng, PhD, my senior brother priest who shared with me his positive personal experience with Christian Faith Publishing.

Finally, I am grateful to bereaved families and friends, especially the Kmeta-Suarez family and Diana Asonaba Dapaah, Esq., and many countless parishioners who shared with opened hearts, their grief, pains, sorrows, and anxiety with me. You are the only reason why I wrote this book. May the courage and burden of sharing your pain with me turn into blessings for others.

Foreword

Human beings have been striving to survive and flourish in the face of death and suffering throughout history. And so it is today. As a devastating pandemic spreads over the world, it adds to the suffering already affecting the planet. Wars, genocides, refugee crises, and torture regimes exist. Devastating poverty afflicts billions. Fires, floods, hurricanes, and famines stem from climate change. And of course, all the monumental disasters interrelate and coexist with the personal sorrows arising from the loss of loved ones to death and a host of other ills. Accidents, injustices, and crimes take their toll. But still evil and woe are never the whole stories of humankind. Humans have survived and flourished because always and everywhere love, altruism, music, art, joy, and intelligence abound.

Religious faiths and rituals have inspired culture and cooperation and still do. Worship inspires and comforts. Faith generates hope, charity and hard work for the welfare of self and others. Humanity, despite setbacks and disasters, has made slow progress toward moral ideals of justice and equality. This journey testifies to the dynamism of our wounded but God-given creation.

Christians have faith that God in Christ has come and won the salvation of the world. Christ embodies God's truth and love, is rejected and put to death, rises from the dead, and will come again. He conquers death and makes all things new. He sends us to proclaim the Gospel—Good News with the power of the Holy Spirit, who empowers us as disciples to fulfill God's loving will that Christ has won for us. So for a Christian, the watchword is "already but not yet." The victory of love and truth over death has been won. We experience joy and hope in the Gospel—Good News—even as we still suffer and die. Faith, love, and hope inspire works of loving service. Healing the world goes on, ever-renewing ourselves in the love of Christ our head. Yes, slowly, we grow up to our Savior and Good Shepherd.

In Vatican II's recent Ecumenical Council call to renew the Church, it proclaims Christians as being on pilgrimage as a learning church. The church learns from and cooperates with people of goodwill. The other purpose of the council was to retrieve the rich resources of Christian tradition to serve the goal of renewal better. The value of Scripture for Christian living was stressed. We seek to discern and follow God's will ever more fully; we can draw on our past riches and learn from new resources of value.

Fr. Thomas in this book has brought both old and new insights to the Old Testament story of Ruth and Naomi to help Christians in this time of world suffering. He draws on modern scientific resources and findings along with traditional theological insights. Fr. Thomas also expands the focus of what the story teaches to larger concerns the world is facing today. The story is founded on ancient Hebrew customs but even more includes universal human relationships and challenges that we recognize today. Ruth and Naomi are heroines and valiant women to emulate. They triumph over suffering and overcome misfortune by faith, initiative, and hard work. Familiar themes of our day appear—such as interracial marriage, widowhood, in-law relations, famine, migration, poverty and remarriage, motherhood and grandmotherhood along with financial security—are the final reward for these virtuous women. This is a story with a happy ending with the joyful reward of the just and the good. But then isn't this a preview of the Gospel—Good News of Christianity?

Since suffering can be psychological and a form of emotional pain and consciousness, it can be caused by sin and immoral mental states. Think of the rage of the wicked when their will is frustrated or jealousy's wrath. The deadly sins bring suffering in their wake. An inordinate self-willed desire is unfulfilled, and others are made to suffer. At another pole of human suffering is its transformation into altruism or sacrifice. Suffering for another or others or righteousness and the good is a universal human occurrence through history; our species has survived and flourished through the altruism of families and social groups. Both pain and emotional suffering for others have brought us the progress we have made.

The sacrificial struggle for others in and out of families can be physically intense but is not unwilling but chosen despite the cost. I choose to act for this good cause, with others or by myself. I do so with satisfaction and sometimes with love and joy. Different emotions can be felt together at different levels or in rapid succession. The support of others is credibly important. Yet our greatest heroes, saints, and martyrs, their suffering has been alone. Christians commemorate the suffering and death of Jesus and meditate on its meaning and saving effect on the world. The most physically agonizing death was combined with conscious suffering.

Sidney Callahan, PhD

Introduction to the Book of Ruth

The book of Ruth in the Old Testament of the Bible is a short drama. It has three key actors and four minor characters. The major actors are Naomi, Ruth, and Boaz; and the minors are Elimelech, Mahlon, Chilion, and Orpah. Naomi and Ruth are the two heroines of a tragic family story that ended triumphantly. Boaz is the hero of the story whose intervention and redemption changed the life of Naomi and Ruth. There is an unnamed supporting character referenced as the kinsman of Elimelech.

The book of Ruth begins with a Jewish couple Elimelech and Naomi. They were from Bethlehem in Judah, which is in the present-day West Bank. Because of famine, they migrated to Moab, which is currently Jordan. Mahlon and Chilion were the two sons of Elimelech and Naomi. Ruth was married to Mahlon, and Orpah to Chilion. Elimelech, Mahlon, and Chilion died unexpectedly. The three men's tragic deaths left three widowed women: Naomi, Ruth, and Orpah.

Boaz entered the final stage of the drama and married Ruth. They gave birth to Obed. The family drama that began sadly ended joyfully with four characters: Naomi, Ruth, Boaz, and Obed. Later, Obed became the father of Jesse, and Jesse became the father of David. Subsequently, Ruth became the great-grandmother of David and the remote ancestress of Jesus of Nazareth, the Christ (Matthew 1:5–6).

The book of Ruth is among the only three books of the Old Testament named after women—Ruth, Esther, and Judith. It is a fascinating short story. It has only four chapters. According to experts, it has only 2,029 words in its original Hebrew language word count through Logos Bible Software.[1]

The Revised Standard Version of the Bible, Catholic Edition (1993) Microsoft word count is 2,775 words. It takes about twenty-five to thirty minutes for a slow reader to read the entire book of Ruth. I strongly encourage you to read the book of Ruth to understand and appreciate this fantastic book. For easier accessibility, I have included the entire text of Ruth before my reflection.

Why this book?

I bought a Holy Bible from amazon.com as my personal Easter gift. The day the Bible was delivered, I was on my way to the basement of the rectory to use the treadmill for my routine weekly exercise. I opened the book of Ruth and started reading it as I have never read it before. I never paid much attention to this book. It appeared that it was my first time reading the book of Ruth. My first thought was to write a leadership book using Naomi as a model of a woman's leadership.

As a priest, a canon lawyer, and a secular law student graduate, I live by textual analysis and interpretation of written documents. My life is anchored on interpreting a biblical text, a canon of the Code of Canon Law, a constitutional provision from a written constitution. As a priest, the primary source of authority for my faith is the Bible. As a canon lawyer, the 1983 Code of Canon Law is authority. Being a law student, a constitution, statutory enactment, and case law are indispensable for lawyering. When I read the book of Ruth, I searched and sought to make sense of the story for myself and others. I was particularly struck by the tragedy and triumph of Naomi and Ruth.

For the last fifteen years of my priestly ministry, I have shared the pains of others. I have heard the constant and consistent question from people of faith; "why is this happening to me?" However,

---

[1] Jeffrey Kranz, Overviewbible.com, https://overviewbible.com/shortest-books/, retrieved June 8, 2020

I have never seen such collective pain, anguish, sadness, and sorrow as during the peak of COVID-19. In the deadly pandemic height, I responded to phone calls from parishioners who were bereaved and from funeral home directors who needed a priest to do a committal service at the cemetery. Often, the voice at the end of the phone was shaking and choked with pain and powerlessness.

I listened with attention and visualized the agony of bereaved families who couldn't have a healthy way of mourning. I had to live-stream committals from cemeteries into the homes of bereaved families because they couldn't come to the graveside due to COVID-19 restrictions. I felt their pain. I found myself sometimes crying alone, especially during my prayer time in the silent and emptied church of St. Matthew in Hastings-on-Hudson in the state of New York. Sometimes, I felt so small and afraid of being in the church alone up to midnight. I had to remind myself that there is no securer place than being in the presence of the Lord in the church at the dark and silent night. I asked the Lord and myself what I can do for these Christian families who call upon me in their grief.

First, I thought of writing a letter to God, expressing my anger and powerlessness, and ask Him to do something for His perishing children. Second, I thought of writing letters to each family, promising them of my prayers and pastoral support. Then I received a letter from a grieving family that reinforced my desire to do something to help. It was a personal letter. It was handwritten. The entire family signed it, thanking me for supporting them in their grief. After reading the letter several times with tears, I decided to write back to this family and other families on how they can grieve as Christians. Essentially, this book is my little contribution to help those who mourn. I believe the story of Ruth may help those grieving for their loss.

I have tried to explore the relevance and resonance of the story as lessons for today's reader. The lessons go beyond grieving to perennial human problems. This book is not a technical biblical analysis or scholarly work but a practical and straightforward application of Ruth's book to specific daily struggles of a believer. It is more or less a Lectio Divina reading of Scripture. Because this book is a personal reflection, I intentionally avoided consulting commentaries and books about Ruth.

After the first draft, I decided to order six books about the book of Ruth to compare what I have written with other literature. I was amazed to see how two people can think alike and use certain common words to express their thoughts. To enrich this book, I have quoted and credited preceding authors: Michelle McClain-Walters, *The Ruth Anointing* (2018); Carolyn Custis James, *Finding God in the Margins* (2018); Sinclair B. Ferguson, *Faithful God: An Exposition of the Book of Ruth* (2013); and Robert L. Hubbard, Jr., *The Book of Ruth* (1998).

The Book of Ruth[2]

Elimelech's Family Goes to Moab

1 In the days when the judges ruled, there was a famine in the land, and a certain man of Bethlehem in Judah went to live in the country of Moab, he and his wife and two sons. [2] The name of the man was Elimelech and the name of his wife Naomi, and the names of his two sons were Mahlon and Chilion; they were Ephrathites from Bethlehem in Judah. They went into the country of Moab and remained there. [3] But Elimelech, the husband of Naomi, died, and she was left with her two sons. [4] These took Moabite wives; the name of the one was Orpah and the name of the other Ruth. When they had lived there about ten years, [5] both Mahlon and Chilion also died, so that the woman was left without her two sons and her husband.

Naomi and Her Moabite Daughters-in-Law

[6] Then she started to return with her daughters-in-law from the country of Moab, for she had heard in the country of Moab that the LORD had considered his people and given them food. [7] So she set out from the place where she had been living, she and her two daughters-in-law, and they went on their way to go

[2] New Revised Standard Version Catholic Edition (NRSVCE) New Revised Standard Version Bible: Catholic Edition, copyright © 1989, 1993 the Division of Christian Education of the National Council of the Churches of Christ in the United States of America. Used by permission. All rights reserved. https://www.biblegateway.com/passage/?search=Ruth+1&version=NRSVCE

back to the land of Judah. [8] But Naomi said to her two daughters-in-law, "Go back each of you to your mother's house. May the LORD deal kindly with you, as you have dealt with the dead and with me. [9] The LORD grant that you may find security, each of you in the house of your husband." Then she kissed them, and they wept aloud. [10] They said to her, "No, we will return with you to your people." [11] But Naomi said, "Turn back, my daughters, why will you go with me? Do I still have sons in my womb that they may become your husbands? [12] Turn back, my daughters, go your way, for I am too old to have a husband. Even if I thought there was hope for me, even if I should have a husband tonight and bear sons, [13] would you then wait until they were grown? Would you then refrain from marrying? No, my daughters, it has been far more bitter for me than for you, because the hand of the LORD has turned against me." [14] Then they wept aloud again. Orpah kissed her mother-in-law, but Ruth clung to her.

[15] So she said, "See, your sister-in-law has gone back to her people and to her gods; return after your sister-in-law." [16] But Ruth said,

> "Do not press me to leave you
>   or to turn back from following you!
> Where you go, I will go;
>   where you lodge, I will lodge;
> your people shall be my people,
>   and your God my God.
> [17] Where you die, I will die—
>   there will I be buried.
> May the LORD do thus and so to me,
>   and more as well,
> if even death parts me from you!"

[18] When Naomi saw that she was determined to go with her, she said no more to her.

[19] So the two of them went on until they came to Bethlehem. When they came to Bethlehem, the whole town was stirred

because of them; and the women said, "Is this Naomi?" [20] She said to them,

> "Call me no longer Naomi,[a][3]
>> call me Mara,[b][4]
>> for the Almighty[c][5] has dealt bitterly with me.
> [21] I went away full,
>> but the LORD has brought me back empty;
> why call me Naomi
>> when the LORD has dealt harshly with[d][6] me,
>> and the Almighty[e][7] has brought calamity upon me?"

[22] So Naomi returned together with Ruth the Moabite, her daughter-in-law, who came back with her from the country of Moab. They came to Bethlehem at the beginning of the barley harvest.

Ruth Meets Boaz

2 Now Naomi had a kinsman on her husband's side, a prominent rich man, of the family of Elimelech, whose name was Boaz. 2 And Ruth the Moabite said to Naomi, "Let me go to the field and glean among the ears of grain, behind someone in whose sight I may find favor." She said to her, "Go, my daughter." 3 So she went. She came and gleaned in the field behind the reapers. As it happened, she came to the part of the field belonging to Boaz, who was of the family of Elimelech. 4 Just then Boaz came from Bethlehem. He said to the reapers, "The LORD be with you." They answered, "The LORD bless you." 5 Then Boaz said to his servant who was in charge of the reapers, "To whom does this young woman belong?" 6 The servant who was in charge of the reapers answered, "She is the Moabite who came back with Naomi from the country of Moab. 7 She said, 'Please, let me glean and gather

---

3   Ruth 1:20 That is Pleasant
4   Ruth 1:20 That is Bitter
5   Ruth 1:20 Traditional rendering of Heb Shaddai,
6   Ruth 1:21 Or has testified against,
7   Ruth 1:21 Traditional rendering of Heb Shaddai.

among the sheaves behind the reapers.' So she came, and she has been on her feet from early this morning until now, without resting even for a moment."[a]8

8 Then Boaz said to Ruth, "Now listen, my daughter, do not go to glean in another field or leave this one, but keep close to my young women. 9 Keep your eyes on the field that is being reaped, and follow behind them. I have ordered the young men not to bother you. If you get thirsty, go to the vessels and drink from what the young men have drawn." 10 Then she fell prostrate, with her face to the ground, and said to him, "Why have I found favor in your sight, that you should take notice of me, when I am a foreigner?" 11 But Boaz answered her, "All that you have done for your mother-in-law since the death of your husband has been fully told me, and how you left your father and mother and your native land and came to a people that you did not know before. 12 May the LORD reward you for your deeds, and may you have a full reward from the LORD, the God of Israel, under whose wings you have come for refuge!" 13 Then she said, "May I continue to find favor in your sight, my lord, for you have comforted me and spoken kindly to your servant, even though I am not one of your servants."

14 At mealtime Boaz said to her, "Come here, and eat some of this bread, and dip your morsel in the sour wine." So she sat beside the reapers, and he heaped up for her some parched grain. She ate until she was satisfied, and she had some left over. 15 When she got up to glean, Boaz instructed his young men, "Let her glean even among the standing sheaves, and do not reproach her. 16 You must also pull out some handfuls for her from the bundles, and leave them for her to glean, and do not rebuke her."

17 So she gleaned in the field until evening. Then she beat out what she had gleaned, and it was about an ephah of barley. 18 She picked it up and came into the town, and her mother-in-law saw how much she had gleaned. Then she took out and gave

---

8   Ruth 2:7 Compare Gk Vg: Meaning of Heb uncertain

her what was left over after she herself had been satisfied. 19 Her mother-in-law said to her, "Where did you glean today? And where have you worked? Blessed be the man who took notice of you." So she told her mother-in-law with whom she had worked, and said, "The name of the man with whom I worked today is Boaz." 20 Then Naomi said to her daughter-in-law, "Blessed be he by the LORD, whose kindness has not forsaken the living or the dead!" Naomi also said to her, "The man is a relative of ours, one of our nearest kin."[b]9 21 Then Ruth the Moabite said, "He even said to me, 'Stay close by my servants, until they have finished all my harvest.'" 22 Naomi said to Ruth, her daughter-in-law, "It is better, my daughter, that you go out with his young women, otherwise you might be bothered in another field." 23 So she stayed close to the young women of Boaz, gleaning until the end of the barley and wheat harvests; and she lived with her mother-in-law.

Ruth and Boaz at the Threshing Floor

3 Naomi her mother-in-law said to her, "My daughter, I need to seek some security for you, so that it may be well with you. 2 Now here is our kinsman Boaz, with whose young women you have been working. See, he is winnowing barley tonight at the threshing floor. 3 Now wash and anoint yourself, and put on your best clothes and go down to the threshing floor; but do not make yourself known to the man until he has finished eating and drinking. 4 When he lies down, observe the place where he lies; then, go and uncover his feet and lie down; and he will tell you what to do." 5 She said to her, "All that you tell me I will do."

6 So she went down to the threshing floor and did just as her mother-in-law had instructed her. 7 When Boaz had eaten and drunk, and he was in a contented mood, he went to lie down at the end of the heap of grain. Then she came stealthily and uncovered his feet, and lay down. 8 At midnight the man was startled, and turned over, and there, lying at his feet, was

---

9 Ruth 2:20 Or one with the right to redeem

a woman! 9 He said, "Who are you?" And she answered, "I am Ruth, your servant; spread your cloak over your servant, for you are next-of-kin."[a]10 10 He said, "May you be blessed by the LORD, my daughter; this last instance of your loyalty is better than the first; you have not gone after young men, whether poor or rich. 11 And now, my daughter, do not be afraid, I will do for you all that you ask, for all the assembly of my people know that you are a worthy woman. 12 But now, though it is true that I am a near kinsman, there is another kinsman more closely related than I. 13 Remain this night, and in the morning, if he will act as next-of-kin[b]11 for you, good; let him do it. If he is not willing to act as next-of-kin[c]12 for you, then, as the LORD lives, I will act as next-of-kin[d]13 for you. Lie down until the morning."

14 So she lay at his feet until morning, but got up before one person could recognize another; for he said, "It must not be known that the woman came to the threshing floor." 15 Then he said, "Bring the cloak you are wearing and hold it out." So she held it, and he measured out six measures of barley, and put it on her back; then he went into the city. 16 She came to her mother-in-law, who said, "How did things go with you,[e]14 my daughter?" Then she told her all that the man had done for her, 17 saying, "He gave me these six measures of barley, for he said, 'Do not go back to your mother-in-law empty-handed.'" 18 She replied, "Wait, my daughter, until you learn how the matter turns out, for the man will not rest, but will settle the matter today."

The Marriage of Boaz and Ruth

4 No sooner had Boaz gone up to the gate and sat down there than the next-of-kin,[a]15 of whom Boaz had spoken, came pass-

---

10 Ruth 3:9 Or one with the right to redeem
11 Ruth 3:13 Or one with the right to redeem
12 Ruth 3:13 Or one with the right to redeem
13 Ruth 3:13 Or one with the right to redeem
14 Ruth 3:16 Or "Who are you,
15 Ruth 4:1 Or one with the right to redeem

ing by. So Boaz said, "Come over, friend; sit down here." And he went over and sat down. 2 Then Boaz took ten men of the elders of the city, and said, "Sit down here"; so they sat down. 3 He then said to the next-of-kin,[b]16 "Naomi, who has come back from the country of Moab, is selling the parcel of land that belonged to our kinsman Elimelech. 4 So I thought I would tell you of it, and say: Buy it in the presence of those sitting here, and in the presence of the elders of my people. If you will redeem it, redeem it; but if you will not, tell me, so that I may know; for there is no one prior to you to redeem it, and I come after you." So he said, "I will redeem it." 5 Then Boaz said, "The day you acquire the field from the hand of Naomi, you are also acquiring Ruth[c]17 the Moabite, the widow of the dead man, to maintain the dead man's name on his inheritance." 6 At this, the next-of-kin[d]18 said, "I cannot redeem it for myself without damaging my own inheritance. Take my right of redemption yourself, for I cannot redeem it."

7 Now this was the custom in former times in Israel concerning redeeming and exchanging: to confirm a transaction, the one took off a sandal and gave it to the other; this was the manner of attesting in Israel. 8 So when the next-of-kin[e]19 said to Boaz, "Acquire it for yourself," he took off his sandal. 9 Then Boaz said to the elders and all the people, "Today you are witnesses that I have acquired from the hand of Naomi all that belonged to Elimelech and all that belonged to Chilion and Mahlon. 10 I have also acquired Ruth the Moabite, the wife of Mahlon, to be my wife, to maintain the dead man's name on his inheritance, in order that the name of the dead may not be cut off from his kindred and from the gate of his native place; today you are witnesses." 11 Then all the people who were at the gate, along with the elders, said, "We are witnesses. May the LORD make the woman who is coming into your house like Rachel and Leah, who together built up the house of Israel. May you produce children

---

16 Ruth 4:5 OL Vg: Heb from the hand of Naomi and from Ruth
17 Ruth 4:3 Or one with the right to redeem
18 Ruth 4:6 Or one with the right to redeem
19 Ruth 4:8 Or one with the right to redeem

in Ephrathah and bestow a name in Bethlehem; 12 and, through the children that the LORD will give you by this young woman, may your house be like the house of Perez, whom Tamar bore to Judah."

The Genealogy of David

13 So Boaz took Ruth and she became his wife. When they came together, the LORD made her conceive, and she bore a son. 14 Then the women said to Naomi, "Blessed be the LORD, who has not left you this day without next-of-kin;[f][20] and may his name be renowned in Israel! 15 He shall be to you a restorer of life and a nourisher of your old age; for your daughter-in-law who loves you, who is more to you than seven sons, has borne him." 16 Then Naomi took the child and laid him in her bosom, and became his nurse. 17 The women of the neighborhood gave him a name, saying, "A son has been born to Naomi." They named him Obed; he became the father of Jesse, the father of David.

18 Now these are the descendants of Perez: Perez became the father of Hezron, 19 Hezron of Ram, Ram of Amminadab, 20 Amminadab of Nahshon, Nahshon of Salmon, 21 Salmon of Boaz, Boaz of Obed, 22 Obed of Jesse, and Jesse of David.

---

[20] Ruth 4:14 Or one with the right to redeem

1

The Common Challenges
of Naomi and Ruth

*In the days when the judges ruled there was a famine in
the land, and a certain man of Bethlehem in Judah went
to sojourn in the country of Moab, he and his wife and
his two sons. The name of the man was Elim'elech and
the name of his wife Na'omi, and the names of his two
sons were Mahlon and Chil'ion; they were Eph'rathites
from Bethlehem in Judah. They went into the country of
Moab and remained there. But Elim'elech, the husband
of Na'omi, died, and she was left with her two sons. These
took Moabite wives; the name of the one was Orpah and
the name of the other Ruth. They lived there about ten
years; and both Mahlon and Chil'ion died, so that the
woman was bereft of her two sons and her husband.*

—Ruth 1:1–5

a. The loss of husbands

Naomi and Ruth's husbands died. Naomi lost Elimelech; Ruth
lost Mahlon. Ruth was a young married lady. The loss of Mahlon is
beyond description. Being a widow at the time was difficult. Even

today, it is still a painful experience. Naomi did not only lose her husband but also her two sons. Naturally, Naomi grieved for the loss of a husband and the two sons. A mother burying her only two sons is something you wouldn't even wish for your worst enemy. Some people never recover from it. It is a devastating experience. It is hellish. It is horrible.

b. They were immigrants

Naomi was an immigrant in Moab. Naomi and her husband migrated from Bethlehem, which is in the present-day West Bank, to Moab, which is in present-day Jordan. Naomi's family came from Bethlehem to Moab because they ran away from hunger. Ruth also became an immigrant when she decided to follow Naomi back to Bethlehem out of faith. Being a foreigner seeking opportunities was challenging. It is still a daunting experience. The difficulties immigrants go through have been well-documented in various migration studies, movies, books, arts, and documentaries. Like many migrants, Naomi and her family were in Moab in search of a better life, yet she met a hellish life. Immigrants derived support from their family and friends. For Naomi to lose her immediate family members was an excruciating experience.

c. They were women

Naomi and Ruth were women in a patriarchal society. They were women in a society built upon family or tribal allegiance with men in charge. A woman's dignity was not respected in many ways. Some people even considered women as part of their properties. Their voices did not count much in some basic decisions about their lives.[21] There is nothing wrong being a woman, but some cultural practices have made being a woman a challenge.

---

[21] Carolyn Custis James, *Finding God in the Margins,* Lexham Press, WA, 2018, 9.

d. They were widows

When Naomi lost Mahlon and Chilion, she became a childless mother. I believe that as many mothers, the two sons were her pride and joy. Ruth did not have a child with Mahlon before his death. Therefore, she was a childless wife. There were three important people in the life of Naomi: her husband and two sons. All of a sudden, three of the four nuclear family members were dead. Naomi was left with only her two daughters-in-law. It was a tragic story. Naomi and Ruth had no children in a society where the best, if not the only, insurance in advanced age was your children. I am not suggesting that being childless or a widow is evil in itself, but in the context of Naomi and Ruth, it meant they could be subject to hunger, abuse, and extreme poverty.

The Lessons

1. Despite Naomi and Ruth's troubles, being widows, without children, poor women, and immigrants, they sailed through these storms with faith, hope, and love. The story of Naomi and Ruth is a drama that is laced with faith in the face of all the reasons to be afraid, hope amid hopeless events, and love despite disappointments. They clung to their faith. They had an unwavering hope that held them together. They loved themselves. They loved each other, and that helped them overcome their adversities. These three virtues propelled these two great women. I submit that their values and virtues, character, and common vision make them heroines and good teachers of dealing with loss.

2. They had a difficult past, yet they made good and great choices to work together. Their resilience in dealing with their loss is exemplary and legendary. In a patriarchal society, Ruth and Naomi made a name for themselves. The transition from the tragedies of life to triumph was not occasioned by chance but by the good choices of these two great women. They had bitter experiences, but they made better choices. Naomi and Ruth

faced the same or similar tragedies, but Naomi became a mentor for Ruth to make the best choices out of their tragedies. They were in the same situation, but Naomi was the leader. Naomi helped Ruth to transform their common loss and worst experiences into the best that life could offer them.

3. They made bold choices and decisions that are worth emulating. They had reasons to be anxious or angry, bitter or brokenhearted, depressed or distressed, wailers and whiners, mourn from morning to evening and cry from dawn to dusk. They surely had grounds to complain and curse about how unfair life was. They made better choices amid the tragedies. Their choices are fascinating. They offer great lessons for us today. Their choices made the world better. They are choices that could make our world better today after this deadly virus that has devastated our world in 2020.

4. We can glean and learn from Naomi and Ruth's principles in dealing with our past, in general, and our painful loss in particular. They teach us that the cure to fear is not courage but faith. Courage is a fruit of faith. Courage begins with faith to fight, to move on, to try, to explore, to write a new story, and to dare to dream. We can learn from how these women who didn't rant but ran the race to the end. They embraced their challenges and persevered toward their goal for a better life. Below are the choices they made out of which we can learn from.

2

They Grieved

Naturally, the death of a loved one leads to grief. Naomi and Ruth grieved. There are various ways people grieve. Culture plays a role in grieving. It may not be anachronistic to suggest that Naomi, Ruth, and Orpah probably went through some of the six stages of grief that Kübler-Ross and Kessler (2014) have espoused namely denial,[22] anger,[23] bargaining,[24]

---

[22] In the first stage, denial "the world becomes meaningless and overwhelming. Life makes no sense. We are in a state of shock and denial. We go numb. We wonder how we can go on, if we can go on, why we should go on. We try to find a way to simply get through each day. Denial and shock help us to cope and make survival possible. Denial helps us to pace our feelings of grief. There is a grace in denial".

[23] In the second stage is anger and it "is a necessary stage of the healing process. Be willing to feel your anger, even though it may seem endless. The more you truly feel it, the more it will begin to dissipate and the more you will heal. There are many other emotions under the anger and you will get to them in time, but anger is the emotion we are most used to managing. The truth is that anger has no limits. It can extend not only to your friends, the doctors, your family, yourself and your loved one who died, but also to God. You may ask, "Where is God in this? Underneath anger is pain, your pain. It is natural to feel deserted and abandoned, but we live in a society that fears anger. Anger is strength and it can be an anchor, giving temporary structure to the nothingness of loss".

[24] The third stage is bargaining. Bargaining "may take the form of a temporary truce. "What if I devote the rest of my life to helping others. Then can I wake up and realize this has all been a bad dream?" We become lost in a maze of "If only…" or "What if…" statements. We want life returned to what is was;

depression,[25] acceptance,[26] and meaning.[27] These six stages are obviously not systematic for everyone. Moreover, people grieve differently and may experience these stages in varied ways.

Naomi, Ruth, and Orpah wept. The three women expressed their emotions. Naomi kissed her daughters-in-law, and *"they lifted up their voices and wept"* (Ruth 1:9). For the second time, *"they lifted up their voices and wept again"* (Ruth 1:14). You can imagine the flood of tears among these three women. They didn't hide their grief. They manifested it by weeping and wailing. The good news is that they didn't cry forever. They accepted the reality of the death of their loved ones. They moved past the tears and pain of bereavement and sought meaning after grieving.

---

we want our loved one restored. We want to go back in time: find the tumor sooner, recognize the illness more quickly, stop the accident from happening… if only, if only, if only. Guilt is often bargaining's companion. The "if onlys" cause us to find fault in ourselves and what we "think" we could have done differently".

[25] The fourth stage is depression. This form of "depression is not a sign of mental illness. It is the appropriate response to a great loss. We withdraw from life, left in a fog of intense sadness, wondering, perhaps, if there is any point in going on alone? Why go on at all? Depression after a loss is too often seen as unnatural: a state to be fixed, something to snap out of. The first question to ask yourself is whether or not the situation you're in is actually depressing. The loss of a loved one is a very depressing situation, and depression is a normal and appropriate response. To not experience depression after a loved one dies would be unusual".

[26] The fifth stage is acceptance. It is important not to confuse acceptance to the idea that it "is "all right" or "OK" with what has happened. This is not the case. Most people don't ever feel OK or all right about the loss of a loved one. This stage is about accepting the reality that our loved one is physically gone and recognizing that this new reality is the permanent reality. We will never like this reality or make it OK, but eventually we accept it. We learn to live with it. It is the new norm with which we must learn to live". Elisabeth Kübler-Ross and David Kessler, *On Grief and Grieving: Finding the Meaning of Grief Through the Five Stages of Loss*, 2014.

[27] David Kessler, *Finding Meaning: The Sixth Stage of Grief*, 2019.

The Lessons

1. To cry is not a sign of weakness. The shortest verse in the English Bible is John 11:35 with only three words, "And Jesus wept." Some translations omit *and* so just two words, "Jesus wept." Jesus was a strong man, yet he cried. He wept for the loss of his friend Lazarus. He had power, and indeed, He raised Lazarus back to life, yet He wept for his death. Weeping is human. It is not a sign of weakness. It is a sign of love for life. We were created to live and not to die. This is the basic reason why we weep at the demise of human life.

2. Weeping is healthy. There are health benefits for reasonable shedding of tears. This is not a suggestion that excessive crying is healthy. It could be a sign of sickness that needs medical care. However, various studies by researchers indicate that crying has health benefits. Science has confirmed that what Naomi and Ruth did was normal and healthy.

The *Medical News Today*, which is part of Healthline Media UK—a credible medical research organization—recently published an article about the health benefits of crying. The article is not only a scientific validation of what Naomi and the two daughters-in-law did, but also it teaches us the health benefits of crying. Here is the entire article about the eight benefits of shedding tears:

> 1. Has a soothing effect
>   Self-soothing is when people: regulate their own emotions[,] calm themselves [and] reduce their own distress[.] A 2014 study found that crying may have a direct, self-soothing effect on people. The study explained how crying activates the parasympathetic nervous system (PNS), which helps people relax.

2.   Gets support from others

As this 2016 study explains, crying is primarily an attachment behavior, as it rallies support from the people around us. This is known as an interpersonal or social benefit.

3.   Helps to relieve pain

Research has found that in addition to being self-soothing, shedding emotional tears releases oxytocin and endorphins. These chemicals make people feel good and may also ease both physical and emotional pain. In this way, crying can help reduce pain and promote a sense of well-being.

4.   Enhances mood

Crying may help lift people's spirits and make them feel better. As well as relieving pain, oxytocin and endorphins can help improve mood. This is why they are often known as "feel good" chemicals.

5.   Releases toxins and relieves stress

When humans cry in response to stress, their tears contain a number of stress hormones and other chemicals. Researchers believe that crying could reduce the levels of these chemicals in the body, which could, in turn, reduce stress. More research is needed into this area, however, to confirm this.

6.   Aids sleep

A small study in 2015 found that crying can help babies sleep better. Whether crying has the same sleep-enhancing effect on adults is yet to be researched. However, it follows that the calming, mood-enhancing, and pain-relieving effects of crying above may help a person fall asleep more easily.

7.   Fights bacteria

Crying helps to kill bacteria and keep the eyes clean as tears contain a fluid called lysozyme. A 2011 study found that lysozyme had such powerful antimicrobial properties that it could even help to reduce risks presented by bioterror agents, such as anthrax.

8.   Improves vision

Basal tears, which are released every time a person blinks, help to keep the eyes moist and prevent mucous membranes from drying out. As the National Eye Institute explains, the lubricating effect of basal tears helps people to see more clearly. When the membranes dry out, vision can become blurry.[28]

---

[28] Eight benefits of crying: Why it's good to shed a few tears, https://www.medicalnewstoday.com/articles/319631 retrieved April 27, 2020

3

The "Where Is God" Question

A sharp knife can be a destructive weapon in the hands of a murderer, but it can also be an instrument of healing in the hands of a surgeon. Everything depends on the hands that use it...God [works] like a skilled surgeon.

—Sinclair B. Ferguson, *Faithful God: An Exposition of the Book of Ruth*, Wales, 2013, 28

In times of calamity, it is natural for believers to ask, "God, where are you? God, what have I done? God, are you punishing me for my sins or the sins of my family? Oh, God, why me again?" Even nonbelievers use the occasion of natural and moral evil to punch believers and query, "Where is your all-powerful and good God?" The problem of evil and a belief in the loving and Almighty God appears difficult for some people to reconcile. It is one of the stumbling blocks for some people to believe in the compassionate God.

Naomi had her moment of God, where are you? When she and Ruth arrived in Bethlehem, the entire "town was stirred because of them; and the women said, 'Is this Na'omi?' She said to them, 'Do not call me Na'omi, call me Mara, for the Almighty has dealt very bitterly with me. I went away full, and the Lord has brought me back empty. Why call me Na'omi, when the Lord has afflicted me, and the Almighty has brought calamity upon me?'" (Ruth 1:19–21). The name Naomi means "pleasantness," beautiful, and nice, but because of her adversities, she changed her name to Mara, which means "bitter" or sorrow. Surprisingly, Naomi attributed her bitter life to God's punishment, her emptiness as the work of God, her affliction and calamity to God. For Naomi, God caused all her woes. I believe that was Naomi's way of dealing with the question, "God, where are you?"

To be clear, Naomi was a woman of faith. She prayed and believed in God's blessings, so why did she think that God was the cause of all that happened to her? This book will not discuss the problem of pain, evil, and suffering. It only suffices to say that pious women and men throughout centuries had to confront the question, "God, where are you?"

The Lessons

1. It is worthy to note that even when Jesus hung on the cross, He had His "God, where are you?" moment. In fact, "Jesus cried out with a loud voice, 'Eloi, Eloi, lama sabachthani?' which means, 'My God, my God, why have you forsaken me?'" (Mark 15:34). I believe that it was not a question of mistrust. There is nothing wrong questioning God if we ask the question with filial reverence and trust that God will answer in His own time and way. Jesus did not doubt His Father's love for Him, what He said was a prayer of Psalm 22:1: "My God, my God, why have you forsaken me? Why are you so far from helping me, from the words of my groaning?" After this prayer, Jesus commended His spirit into God, the Father's hands.

2. We may experience a moment in our lives when we just don't understand what God is doing with us, and we just can't make sense of what is happening to us. There are personal and historical examples, like the loss of a family member or friend, natural disasters like hurricanes, tsunamis, the Spanish flu, COVID-19, etc. Natural and human-made evil causes us to question our belief in Almighty loving God. We are tempted to think either God is less powerful or less loving. The biggest lesson is that we don't have to be afraid to ask God questions; we have to be

patient. We must wait for the answer, keep the faith while waiting for the answer, and be humble to accept the answer when it finally comes. There are a lot of examples of people of faith asking God questions and faithfully seeking answers in the book of Job (see Job 7:18–21) and in the Psalms (see Psalm 22:1–2).

4

The "What Next" Question

We have a tendency to hold grudges against God and others and not realize how it holds us back from being all that God wants us to be. Some of us have gone through unmentionable loss, betrayals, and challenges, and the initial feelings of hurt, rejection, anger, and sadness were justified to a degree. But where are we now? Have we forgiven? Have we allowed the Lord to heal our hearts?

—Michelle McClain-Walters, *The Ruth Anointing,* Florida, 2018, 62

It is a common cultural practice for family and friends to come together to mourn their loss. I believe that was the prevailing culture at the time of Naomi, Orpah, and Ruth. After the demise of a loved one, the presence of family members and friends is consoling and comforting. It shows compassion and common humanity that when one of us suffers, we all suffer together. In some cultures, flowers, letters, phone calls, e-mails, and text messages are sent to the bereaved family as a sign of solidarity.

In some societies, grieving is not private and personal but public and communal. However, when all is done, the immediate family has to handle their loss privately despite initial communal support. After the burial, the religious rituals, the celebrations, the funeral services, the condolences from friends, and the immediate family have to answer the question, "What next?" The bereaved family must face that existential question of, "How do I move on?"

Lesson

Naomi, Orpah, and Ruth had to deal with the difficult question "What next?" after weeping. For some people, the death of a loved one is the end of life, but for Naomi and Ruth, death was the beginning of a new life. For some people, death brings closure to their world, but for Naomi and Ruth, death opened the door to a new world. For some people, death is darkness, but for Naomi and Ruth, the death of their loved ones became a torchlight to walk and explore beyond the darkness of death. For some people, death is deafness to the beauty of the present, but for Naomi and Ruth, death led them in search of the best of life. They became companions to walk and talk together in search of a deeper meaning of life after loss.

5

Conversation

Then she started with her daughters-in-law to return from the country of Moab, for she had heard in the country of Moab that the LORD had visited his people and given them food. So she set out from the place where she was, with her two daughters-in-law, and they went on the way to return to the land of Judah. But Na'omi said to her two daughters-in-law, "Go, return each of you to her mother's house. May the LORD deal kindly with you, as you have dealt with the dead and with me. The LORD grant that you may find a home, each of you in the house of her husband!" Then she kissed them, and they lifted up their voices and wept.

—Ruth 1:6–9

After the demise of Naomi's husband and two sons, she sat down with Orpah and Ruth for a conversation. To answer the question of what happens next requires leadership. Someone within the family has to lead, initiate, and guide the conversation. Naomi did that. Today, there are many counselors, therapists, priests, rabbis, imams, and social workers who step up to help bereaved families to have conversation after their loss. They aim to assist families, communities, and nations in grieving. Professional help may be necessary and helpful, but individual efforts in meeting professional assistance are indispensable. This is the reason why I submit that Naomi is an example and a teacher for us today. Grief entails conversation, negotiation, discussion, and decision.

a. *They negotiated*

Naomi came to the family conversation table to negotiate. Her first original plan was to return with Ruth and Orpah to Judah. In fact, "she started with her daughters-in-law to return from the country of Moab" to Judah (Ruth 1:6). Along the way, Naomi made a second proposal to Ruth and Orpah. She asked them to "return each of you to her mother's house" (Ruth 1:8). Naomi changed her mind, not out of malice. She was motivated by a sincere concern for them. She wanted Ruth and Orpah to go back, look for husbands, have children, and a better life.

Ruth and Orpah had to negotiate. The initial offer appeared to have been withdrawn by Naomi with a new offer. They had to choose to renegotiate the first offer or take the second offer before them. Each had to make her own choice. They chose to negotiate the first offer when "they said to her, 'No, we will return with you to your people'" (Ruth 1:10). They weren't angry with Naomi for changing her mind but were ready to pursue her to stick to their initial agreement.

Naomi insisted that they turn back and questioned them as to why they have to go with her. Naomi reasoned with them about why she changed her mind. She gave them the reasons why the first offer was not good for them. She told them to turn back because she was "too old to have a husband. If I should say I have hope, even if I should have a husband this night and should bear sons, would you, therefore, wait until they were grown? Would you, therefore, refrain from marrying?" (Ruth 1:12). From their dialogue, it is clear that Naomi had their interest at heart. She wanted nothing but the good of Ruth and Orpah. She was, therefore, prepared to listen to them. Their conversation was driven by mutual understanding and good faith.

b.   *They decided after their discussion*

They had to conclude their discussion with a decision. They were free women who had to make responsible choices for themselves. Orpah decided to go her way. Ruth decided to go with Naomi. They made different choices based on the two offers at the negotiation table. They didn't have to do the same thing. Naomi and Ruth decided to walk together, but Orpah went alone. They had a common tragedy but different means of handling it. They had the same misery but different missions on earth. They had similar difficulties but different pursuits. Ruth took a decision not based on feelings alone but faith. She pledged her loyalty to Naomi.

c.   *They walk the walk*

There was an implementation of their decisions. After their decisions were made from their discussion, they had to walk the walk. Orpah left, then Naomi and Ruth traveled together. They were faithful to their resolutions. Ruth and Orpah understood that every decision requires commitment. Ruth committed herself to her choice. Her decision to follow Naomi required her to abandon her home. She had to venture into a new culture. Naomi had to travel to unknown territory with all the risks. The cost of living up to her decision was not easy, yet Ruth was ready to walk through all the challenges ahead of her. Naomi's acceptance of Ruth to travel with her came with responsibility. She had to mentor a young widow on how to survive in a difficult world.

The Lessons

1.   Naomi did not come to the conversation with a mindset: "this is my offer, take it or leave it." She was ready to listen. She asked them questions that demanded honest answers. She tried to reason with Ruth and Orpah. That is how conversation works. That is how a family, a community, and a nation may learn to handle their loss. Any form of an entrenched position doesn't

help. Unreasonable demands hurt more and aggravate existing pain. Accusations and counteraccusations do not bring healing. There must be a respectful discussion about what next.

2. Their discussion was not about feelings alone but thinking. It was an emotional and rational discussion of three women. Naomi offered compelling reasons why Orpah and Ruth should not follow her to Judah. Ruth reasoned with Naomi as to why she wanted to travel with her. There was no name-calling. There was no imputation of ill motive. They focused on the issue before them, which was the future of their relationships.

3. Their conversation, discussion, and deliberation led to decisions. Naomi, Orpah, and Ruth didn't have endless discussions. At some point, they had to make up their minds, which they did. Decision making is difficult and may not be pleasant but need not be spiteful of others. The lesson for us is that their decision to part company was not acrimonious. Orpah kissed Naomi as a sign of affection and left.

4. Naomi provided the necessary leadership in the conversation. She didn't call Ruth and Orpah to accuse or blame them for something they didn't do but to discuss what is next. Naomi is a great teacher of how to facilitate a meaningful and efficient conversation. Naomi did not use her experience, age, and foresight to impose anything on them but gave them guidelines and directions. Naomi gave both the chance to decide for themselves. Naomi persuaded them to leave her, but she did not pressure them to accept her way as the only way. Naomi did not coerce them but consented to their plans and respective choices.

The lesson is that in a conversation about the future, we don't need to impose our solutions on others but propose them for evaluation. Therefore, Naomi is a model for family conversation, the community healing process, national and international dialogue for post-COVID-19 conversation.

6

They Were United

*Become friends to those who have no friends. Become
family to those who have no family. Become a community to those who have no community. May we all share
what we have with one another as children of the one
God who loves everyone and who offers to everyone the
gift of peace.*

—Pope John Paul II and Durepos
Joseph, *Lessons for Living* (2004)

When Naomi and Ruth decided to stay together, they formed a team.
They realized that a team survives and thrives if there is a change
from "I" to "we." Families, corporations, groups, and nations suc-
ceed in recovering their loss if they come together. That is the lesson
Naomi and Ruth teach us. The road to success demands a transition
from "I" to "we", and from "me" to "us." Naomi and Ruth understood that working together means helping each other as a team. As
a team, they aimed at victory. As a team, their collective success was
their goal.

Naomi and Ruth united to overcome their grief. Therefore,
they refused to be victims and embarked on a journey to success.
They could have cursed God for their hellish misery. They could
have doubted God's existence. They could have questioned God's

unconditional love. They chose a different path to work together as women of faith, hope, and love. I believe it was not an easy choice, but they believed that walking and working together would be successful, which it was indeed.

The Lessons

1. In unity lies strength. Naomi and Ruth saw strength in unity. There is an African proverb that says, "If you want to go fast, go alone, but you want to go far, go together." When Ruth joined forces with Naomi, she went far. She married Boaz, a wealthy and a loving husband. She gave birth to Obed and Obed became the father of Jesse, and Jesse was the father of David (Matthew 1:5–6). She became the ancestress of the famous king David and ancestress of Jesus of Nazareth, whom we Christians unapologetically and firmly believe is the Christ, the Savior of the world.

    Ruth did not ask, "If I stay with Naomi, what will happen to me?" Ruth was concerned about Naomi as much as she was concerned about herself. Her thinking was, we are stronger together. We are better off being together. We are in this together. We are a team. I believe these were the motivations that led Ruth to work together with Naomi. They became successful together. Their legacy lives on.

2. Unity is key to success. With unity, Naomi and Ruth became successful. History teaches us that unity is necessary to overcome adversity. Countries and civilizations have triumphed and survived because of unity. Just look at the United Kingdom and the United States of America. Like these two great countries or loathe them, you can't take away the fact that their unity is their greatest strength. The European Union (EU) project is an example of what unity of purpose can do. With all its problems and challenges, the EU has made Europe and the world stable, peaceful, and prosperous after the cruel and horrific World War II. Indeed, Naomi and Ruth teach us that there is success in unity.

As a team, Naomi helped Ruth to dream again. Naomi helped Ruth to find a new husband. Naomi was not bitter that her daughter-in-law had found another man. She even assisted her in discovering and discerning Boaz as the love of her life. In some cultures, a daughter-in-law suffers all forms of abuse from a mother-in-law after the demise of her husband. There is a malicious presumption that she did not take care of her husband. That wasn't the thinking of Naomi. She was a loving and caring mother-in-law who teamed up with her to find another sweet and suitable husband.

3. In unity, Naomi and Ruth sought meaning after their loss. They were united to make sense out of the nonsense of life. They were women, widows; Naomi was childless mother; and Ruth had no children with her first husband and immigrants; yet none of these defined their destiny or deterred them from succeeding. Naomi decided to return home from a foreign land. Ruth decided to leave home to a foreign land. They teach us how to build bridges. A Moabite woman and a Jewish woman changed the world through unity. Their alliance gave birth to one of the famous kings in the world, David the king of Israel, and Jesus of Nazareth, the King of the universe.

7

They Changed

John Henry Newman once said, "To live is to change and to be perfect is to have changed often."[29] Indeed, change is a necessary part of life, and success demands change. Naomi and Ruth realized that and made the necessary changes according to their particular situation.

They Changed Their Status

Naomi and Ruth changed roles and status. Naomi changed from mother-in-law to mother-in-love. Ruth became a daughter-in-love and not a daughter-in-law. The bond between them was no more about the law but love. Previously, social norms defined their relationship, but the change of status redefined their bond based on faith, hope, love, common aspirations, perseverance, and a search for a better life. As a mother-in-love, Naomi mentored Ruth with such a profound love. Naomi took care of Ruth as a good mother would do. Ruth, in return, took care of Naomi as a good daughter would do. They were not compelled by social mores or norms to take care of one another. They rather lived according to the great commandment of love.

---

[29] John Henry Newman, *An Essay on the Development of Christian Doctrine* (1845), Chapter 1, Section 1, Part 7.

They Changed Their Environment

Naomi, a native of Judah, decided to return home—from Moab to Judah. Ruth, a native of Moab, resolved to leave her home—from Moab to Judah.

The Lessons

1. Through their change of status, Naomi became a mentor and Ruth, a mentee. Naomi coached Ruth. Naomi helped Ruth to discern and discover her future husband, Boaz. As a mentee, Ruth was ready to learn. She followed the directions, instructions, and guidelines of Naomi. Change is difficult because it requires adjustment, experiment, and learning. That explains why Naomi and Ruth's relationship is so important in dealing with loss. It teaches us to be humble and to learn from one another.

2. Naomi and Ruth teach us the reason for a change is important. The values or virtues underpinning change matter. The two women teach us that real change begins from the heart and mind. Change driven by love makes a difference. Naomi and Ruth teach us that the idea of the rule of law needs love. That proposition is not utopian. Because where there is love, there is order; where there is love, there is a responsibility; where there is love, there are respect and reverence for life, liberty, truth, justice, and the pursuit of happiness. Love is the foundation of true law. My biblical scholar friend Fr. Mike asserted that "the soul of the Jewish Law in the Book of Deuteronomy 6:4ff (the Shema) begins with a call to love YHWH." Indeed, where love reigns, hatred fails to ruin people. That is the secret of Naomi and Ruth's success. That is why Naomi changed from mother-in-law to mother-in-love. That is why Ruth changed from daughter-in-law to daughter-in-love. Naomi and Ruth teach us that true leadership in difficult times requires the need and willingness to change to serve others out of love.

If you don't believe that love is the soul of true law, just research about all the nations of the world, their leaders claim to govern by the rule of law. If not all, the majority of the nations on earth have signed on to the International Bill of Human Rights. Yet some leaders have zero understanding and appreciation of the role of love in the rule of law. They don't serve people out of love but out of a rule of law that keeps them in power and makes them more powerful and their citizens more powerless. If love animates the rule of law, a government takes care of the governed, and citizens lack no basic needs of life such as food, clothing, shelter, education, medical care, and basic freedoms.

3. Naomi chose to go back home in Judah when she has lost her immediate family in Moab. With the news that Judah was doing well, she decided to go home. She realized that prosperity is not confined to one place. In Paulo Coelho's novel, *Alchemist*, the protagonist of the story was a shepherd in search of a treasury. In that amazing story, Coelho explains how sometimes the treasures we search outside ourselves are sometimes inside and around us.

    There are stories of migrants who went back home to change the direction of their families and countries. The story of Naomi resonates with migrants who go back home to make a positive impact. Naomi's story connects with the stories of immigrants who have returned home by choice and not through the force of the law of repatriation. The choice of Naomi to return home paid off.

4. Ruth chose to leave home to make it in another part of the world. That was a courageous choice too. Ruth is an example of people who leave their homes to follow their dreams. She is an example of people who leave home in search of opportunities in foreign lands. Some Europeans did it and made it to the United States of America, Brazil, Argentina, Australia, New Zealand, etc. Today, some Africans, South Americans, and Asians are repeating the same history. Indeed, history repeats itself with all the twists and turns, fears, and faith.

Some people leave their homeland. Some people return to their homeland. Ruth and Naomi are an example of how "home" is being with the people you love, who love you, and will always be with you. Orpah is an example of people who you love and who love you but who will nevertheless leave you. It is called a choice—the exercise of one's free will. That is what Naomi, Ruth, and Orpah teach us. The world will be a better place if we can learn from their different choices. The world will be a palace where we will all be kings and queens if we are ready to learn from these amazing women's choices.

5. Naomi and Ruth teach us to dare to dream, to travel, to adventure, to take reasonable risk. Naomi lost almost everything and everyone in a foreign land yet continued to move forward with her life. Ruth similarly suffered a great loss but wasn't afraid to migrate to another foreign land. Ruth did not allow the negative experience of Naomi to prevent her from leaving her land of birth, Moab, to travel to Judah, a foreign land. They were dreamers. The loss of their first dream didn't prevent them from having a second dream.

8

They Shared Sympathy and Empathy

After the death of the loves of their lives, Naomi and Ruth shared a common sympathy and empathy. Ruth sympathized with Naomi for the loss of her husband and her sons; Naomi sympathized with Ruth for the loss of her husband, Mahlon, and the loss of her ability to have any children with him. Therefore, Naomi and Ruth exchanged compassion and consolation. The mutual sympathy and empathy animated their conversation about what is next for them. Shared sympathy and empathy also influenced Ruth and Naomi's decision to travel together.

Sympathy and empathy are about helping people walk their walk in life—to help them "wear their shoes." Indeed, two people cannot wear one shoe at the same time. However, it is also true that when two people walk and work together, one can help the other to remove her shoe if the other is unable to do so alone. In that regard, sympathy and empathy are not just putting yourself in other people's shoes. Instead, they are about helping them get the right shoe, the right size, and wear it fittingly and comfortably.

Sympathy and empathy are not just carrying someone else's cross. Sympathy and empathy are about helping others to embrace their cross. Even Jesus of Nazareth, who invited His followers to take their crosses and follow Him, didn't carry His cross alone. He had the help of Simon of Cyrene to carry His cross to Calvary. Though there were external powers that forced Simon to help Jesus carry the cross, sympathy and empathy are internal powers that propel human beings to help others to carry their cross. They are strong emotional tools that help us to serve one another. They are basic human instincts that enable us to assist others to be on their feet to walk.

Sympathy and empathy enable us to channel our emotional connection of the sufferings of others into charity. They help us to understand the pain of others and work with them to find a solution. Because of sympathy and empathy, Ruth and Naomi might have asked the golden question, "What will happen to the other person if I don't help her?" Ruth might have asked, "What will happen to Naomi, an elderly widow, if I abandon her?" Naomi might have asked the golden question too, "What will happen to Ruth, a young widow who is so determined to travel with me, if I leave her in Moab?"

The Lessons

1. There is strength in shared sympathy and empathy. Naomi and Ruth gained strength to deal with their pain because of their shared compassion. They offer us an example of the power of compassion and solidarity. We need sympathy and empathy in the post-COVID-19 world to deal with the loss of human lives and properties.

2. Sympathy and empathy are tools for transformation. Naomi and Ruth offer us an example of how sympathy and empathy can transform the world. Sympathy and empathy changed their personal story, and they can change ours. We already have an example of how sympathy and empathy shaped postapartheid South Africa.

   After fifty years of Apartheid in South Africa, the Truth and Reconciliation Commission (TRC) under the spirit of sympathy and empathy initiated the healing process, restorative justice, compassion, and forgiveness. Despite the challenges of TRC, it helped in healing the painful past of South Africa.

   I believe sympathy and empathy helped the oppressor and the oppressed in the TRC process. Given what Apartheid did to native South Africans and where they are today, one cannot discount the role of sympathy and empathy in redeeming and healing the hurts and pains of people as they did for South Africans.

9

They Had Faith

How can we profess faith in God's Word, and then refuse to let it inspire and direct our thinking, out activity, our decisions, and our responsibilities toward one another? Faith is always demanding because faith leads us beyond ourselves. Faith imparts a vision of life's purpose and stimulates us to action.

—Pope John Paul II, *Lessons for Living*, 12

Fate is what happens to us without our consent. Faith is what happens with our consent. Faith is a choice. It is a choice to confide in the light when faced with darkness. Naomi and Ruth were women of incredible faith. Faith was their anchor. Ruth took a leap of faith in deciding to go to Judah with Naomi. Ruth was determined to go with Naomi because she loved and trusted her and chose to believe in a personal God. Ruth made a declaration of faith in God, in herself, Naomi, and in humanity. The demonstration of faith in a personal God—who provides and protects His highest creatures, human beings—made all the difference in the life of Naomi and Ruth. They had confidence in themselves and humanity because they had faith in God.

The Lessons

1. Faith was a compass for Naomi and Ruth. With faith, they saw life as a gift to cherish, live, and triumph over adversities. Because of their faith, the deaths of their loved ones didn't bury their dreams. With faith, they set new priorities and prayed for a better life.

2. Faith gives us a mission. In the case of Naomi and Ruth, faith gave them a new mission that was to explore, travel, and help themselves. With faith, they explored God's plan for themselves amid their adversities. Indeed, with faith, Ruth transformed her misfortune into fortune. With faith, deaths did not crush their dreams. Because of their faith, they cried to God for consolation and redemption. With faith, they did not crawl on the altar of sorrow, but they prayed for God's blessings. Naomi and Ruth teach us that with faith, the best of life is ahead of us even when we are faced with worse setbacks.

3. With faith, Naomi and Ruth avoided self-pity and self-victimization. They didn't allow their bitter experience and sorrow to undermine faith in their Creator and themselves. Their troubles did not take away their God-given creativity and potential. In a post-COVID-19 world, like Naomi and Ruth, we need to activate our faith in humanity to build a new family, government, nation, and society.

   It will be another tragedy to waste time blaming government officials, policy makers, politicians, pastors/priests, healthcare professionals, and businessmen and women. That is not to suggest that we shouldn't hold people responsible for their actions and inactions. However, I submit that we can hold people responsible without being resentful and self-pitying. Resentment will not help us. It will hurt us more. We need faith in God, in ourselves, in our shared humanity to fix a broken world.

4. Naomi and Ruth teach us that playing the victim takes away our strength to strive and thrive with faith. Naomi and Ruth teach us that fate is the tragedy that comes to us, but faith is what helps us to respond triumphantly.

10

They Celebrated

There is positive energy in celebration. There is a strength that comes from celebrating the triumphs of others and our own success story. In fact, by celebrating the good efforts of others, we motivate them to bring out the best in themselves. That is what Naomi did for Ruth. Naomi was happy and celebrated when Ruth and Boaz met, fell in love, and married. Naomi rejoiced when Ruth gave birth to Obed. Naomi teaches humanity to celebrate the good things of life. Boaz also celebrated Ruth even before their marriage. Ruth also celebrated both Naomi and Boaz.

The Lessons

1. We need to celebrate our success and the good things that happen to us. Naomi and Ruth grieved their loss, yet they had reason to celebrate the joy of a new life. Naomi and Ruth celebrated each other because there is joy in celebrating others. To celebrate others, you need to see the good in them and the best things they are capable of doing. Naomi and Ruth teach us that if you dwell on the faults of others and what is wrong with them, you cannot celebrate their achievements. For instance, if parents regularly and consistently look at the failures of their children, they cannot praise them. They cannot bring out the good in them. This is true in all relationships. If we look only

at the flaws or faults of others, we cannot celebrate the good in them.

2. Celebrating others is a sign of gratitude. To celebrate others is an indication that you are grateful for who they are to you. Naomi and Ruth kept an attitude of gratitude. There was a mutual display of appreciation for the gift of each other. They respected each other and were grateful for the company of each other. Celebrating others' success is a sign of gratitude. We can learn from Naomi and Ruth by honoring one another.

3. Celebrating others shows we appreciate the good in them. Some people are fixated on the faults of their family, friends, community, church, nation, and the world. Such people complain about everything and contribute nothing to fix anything. The world will be a better place if we can learn to give praise, where praise is due. Naomi is an excellent teacher of how to celebrate others. To those who have all the necessities and luxuries of life but are not grateful for them, may they learn from the example of Naomi and Ruth who were content with the little they had. To those who are never satisfied with the sacrifices of others, Naomi and Ruth teach us that we don't need to solve all our problems to celebrate the good things of life. We sometimes need to put the painful past behind us and celebrate our blessings and gains.

4. Celebrating others softens our daily burdens. When we refuse to celebrate the good things of life, we make life itself burdensome. With the joy of celebration, our challenges become opportunities to use the power of the human will and God's grace to overcome adversity. Naomi and Ruth did not allow their loss to become a barrier in seeking their breakthrough. Naomi and Ruth could have lived their hell on earth, given what they went through, yet they were grateful and content for the good things that came their way. Naomi and Ruth teach us that no matter our loss, we could still find a reason to celebrate the joy of life itself.

11

They Lived the Two Universal Rules

*Instead of dwelling on her own losses, Ruth chose to give
up everything to see about her mother-in-law's welfare,
and in return she received all that she had lost and more.*

—Michelle McClain-Walters

Two basic universal rules govern human beings. They are silver and
golden rules.[30] The silver rule is, "do not do unto others what you
do not want others to do to you." The silver rule restrains you from
harming others. It is about justice. It controls the evil inclinations
in us to undermine and destroy others. The silver rule protects us
against our selfish human nature to pursue personal interests against
the common good.

The golden rule is "to do unto others what is right." The golden
rule commands us to do good. The golden rule compels our con-
science to contribute to improving the lives of others. The golden
rule drives and thrives on good human instincts to help others. The
golden rule is about our shared humanity. The golden rule is about
the activation of what is good in us. It urges us to help others. The
golden rule is about making a positive influence on the lives of oth-

---

[30] Q. C. Terry, *Golden Rules and Silver Rules of Humanity: Universal Wisdom of
Civilization*, 2015

ers. The golden rule is about charity—love; the silver rule is about justice. The golden and silver rules do not contradict each other, but they complement one another.

Naomi and Ruth lived the golden rule because Naomi wanted a husband, children, grandchildren, prosperity, and all the good things of life. But she did not get those things. Naomi helped Ruth to get the very good things of life that she didn't get. Ruth chose to go with Naomi because of the golden rule. Naomi helped Ruth to discern the interest of Boaz in her. The golden rule led Ruth to take care of Naomi by working hard to put food on the table for the two of them.

The Lesson

Naomi and Ruth teach us that instead of restraining from evil, our call is to do good and contribute to building a better world. We need to move away from "I didn't do anything wrong to her" to "I did something good for her." We need to change from "I didn't hurt her" to "I did help her." We need to move away from "I didn't kill her" to "I did care for her."

12

They Were Patient

Patience is endurance. It is the ability to persevere and keep a positive attitude amid all the negatives. Patience is not passive. It is not just waiting for adverse events to pass or saying to yourself "this too shall pass." Patience is the ability to use the spirit of fortitude to fight until the end. It is doing your part and remaining calm, waiting for the results. Patience is taking it one day at a time. It is being at peace while waiting for the fulfillment of a promise or dream. Naomi, Ruth, and Boaz were all patient to the end. Through patience, their dreams came to fruition.

Ruth had to wait for another husband. Naomi had to calm her down after her encounter with Boaz. Naomi said to her, "Wait my daughter, until you learn how the matter turns out, for the man will not rest, but will settle the matter today" (Ruth 3:18). One could reasonably infer that Ruth was eager to accelerate everything with Boaz, but Naomi used her experience to ask her to exercise patience. Here was a young woman who lost her first husband without a child, so you can imagine how she might have been anxiously waiting for a husband and child.

Boaz too had to wait for the performance of the rite of redemption before he could marry Ruth. He patiently followed all the procedures and rituals before he tied the knot with Ruth. Boaz didn't rush to marry Ruth. He didn't use his power and influence without recourse to the custom, rites, procedures outlined for everyman at the time. He prayed to God and played by the rules. He met the elders and did what was expected of him before he finally married Ruth.

The Lessons

1. Love and patience win. Naomi, Ruth, and Boaz took it one day at a time and did the right thing, until their dreams came through. They became victorious through endurance, perseverance, and trust. They teach us the power of love and patience. From their experience, we can learn that with love and patience, victory will come at the right time. We need love and patience to recover from any loss. Love and patience are essential virtues of recovering or restoring what has been destroyed.

2. Patience requires the right attitude. We have to wait for so many things in life. We have to wait to crawl before we walk. After walking then, we have to learn to run. A student has to wait to finish school. After graduation, wait for a job. After employment, wait for building or buying or renting a house, getting a husband or wife and a child. What happens while we are waiting for someone or something is so important. Naomi and Ruth kept faith and trust while waiting. They enjoyed the presence of one another while waiting. They said a prayer of blessing while waiting. They had a constructive family conversation while waiting. These are the lessons we can learn while dealing with any loss. With patience, we shall recover, rebuild, and soar higher.

3. Patience is humbling. It tells us that we can do a lot of things, but we cannot do all things. Patience makes us aware that human beings are powerful, but only God is all-powerful. Therefore, we have to wait for God's time. Patience teaches us that we may know a lot of things and a lot of people, but only God is all-knowing. Therefore, we have to wait for answers to our unanswered questions. With patience, we know that grieving requires humility. With humility, we can accept that we are fragile and sometimes more infantile than we would like to

admit. Sometimes in grieving, we may cry like babies. When it happens, we need to be patient with ourselves. The healing process takes time and has its rhythm.

4. Patience teaches us that God is always faithful, but we may think He is not always fair to us. In times of loss, we may ask ourselves or whisper to God, "This is not fair." We may never understand why this is happening to us, but with patience, one thing will undoubtedly be made known to us, which is God's faithfulness. Indeed, God keeps to His promise, though sometimes it takes longer. We know it was not fair for Joseph to go to prison, but we know with patience, Joseph the prisoner became a "prime minister" of Egypt—a very powerful nation at the time. We know it was not fair for Nelson Mandela to spend twenty-seven years in prison, but we know with endurance, Nelson Mandela, the prisoner, became the president of South Africa. With patience, justice will finally come.

5. Patience shows a person's real character. With patience, we discover our strength, resilience, and fortitude. With patience, we get to know people better and set our priorities right. With endurance, we build a solid character. Patience helps us to know fragile people and those who are fake, vulnerable people, and those who are just vicious, weak people, and those who are wicked. Thus, discerned and discovered, we can help the fragile, fight for the weak, and be a voice for the vulnerable. With patience, we purify our character and know the true character of others.

13

They Prayed

Prayer is not one occupation among many, but is at the center of our life in Christ. It turns our attention away from ourselves and directs it to the Lord. Prayer fills the mind with truth and gives hope to the heat.

—Pope John Paul II, *Lessons for Living*, 43

First, Naomi began her conversation with Ruth and Orpah with a prayer of blessing. She said to them, "May the Lord deal kindly with you, as you have dealt with the dead and with me. The Lord grant that you may find a home, each of you in the house of her husband!" (Ruth 1:9). Naomi recognized the kindness of Ruth and Orpah. Therefore, she invoked God's compassion on the two daughters-in-law by explicitly asking God to bless them with husbands and houses that will be a home for them. Naomi wished them nothing but goodness.

Second, Boaz blessed Ruth when they met for the first time. He said to her, "The Lord recompense you for what you have done, and a full reward be given you by the Lord, the God of Israel, under whose wings you have come to take refuge!" (Ruth 2:12). Boaz said a prayer of blessing for Ruth because of Ruth's kindheartedness to Naomi and her faith in God.

Third, when Ruth returned from the farm and narrated her encounter with Boaz, Naomi blessed Boaz for his gentleness. She said, "Blessed be the man who took notice of you" (Ruth 2:19). Naomi didn't take for granted Boaz's kindness. She prayed for him. She also said a prayer of thanksgiving to God for him. She honored the Lord for His compassion. She said, "Blessed be he by the Lord, whose kindness has not forsaken the living or the dead!" (Ruth 2:20). Despite all her miseries, Naomi found a reason to thank God. We can always find something to be grateful to God for.

Fourth, Boaz blessed and prayed for Ruth when he saw that Ruth was interested in him. Boaz said to Ruth, "May you be blessed by the Lord, my daughter; you have made this last kindness greater than the first, in that you have not gone after young men, whether poor or rich" (Ruth 3:10). Boaz was grateful to God for the gift of Ruth when they had their special moment.

Fifth, at the end of the rite of redemption, the assembly said a prayer of blessings for Boaz and Ruth's marriage. The people and the elders prayed, "May the Lord make the woman, who is coming into your house, like Rachel and Leah, who together built up the house of Israel. May you prosper in Eph'rathah and be renowned in Bethlehem; and may your house be like the house of Perez, whom Tamar bore to Judah, because of the children that the Lord will give you by this young woman" (Ruth 4:11–12). The people desired goodness, greatness, prosperity, and a great legacy for Boaz and Ruth.

Sixth, when Ruth conceived and gave birth to Obed, Naomi's neighbors said a prayer of blessing. They praised God for gifting Naomi with a next of kin. They said, "Blessed be the Lord, who has not left you this day without next of kin; and may his name be renowned in Israel!" (Ruth 4:14). Naomi's neighbors were happy for her and gave thanks to God for granting the wish of Naomi. Above all, they were all grateful for God's goodness.

The Lessons

1. There is a need for prayer in the life of a believer. Prayer is a basic tenet of the Judeo-Christian faith. For Naomi and Boaz,

prayer was an essential part of their faith in God. It comes as no surprise that in all the six instances cited above, Naomi, Boaz, and the community prayed. Prayer was their way of life. As believers in the Judeo-Christian faith, prayer is our way of life too. Prayer is not something we do but something we have. It is our greatest weapon. It is our shield against evil and our sword to do good.

2. There is power in the prayer of intercession. Charity requires that we pray for others and not only for ourselves. That is why Naomi prayed for Ruth and Orpah. Boaz prayed for Ruth. The elders and the community prayed for Boaz and Ruth. Prayer was a great gift that they exchanged and gave to each other. It is time for families to pray together and for one another. It is time to pray for the success of one another. The prayer of blessing restored the loss of Ruth. The prayer of blessing did not restore Naomi's loss, but it gave her peace and joy and a renowned descendant.

3. There is power in the prayer of thanksgiving. Naomi, Boaz, and the community teach us that prayer is not always asking but giving. Through prayer, we give thanks, praise, and glory to God. That is so important. Prayer of thanksgiving is a sign of gratitude. The more we appreciate what God has already given us, the more He showers more blessings upon us.

4. There is power in spoken words. Naomi teaches us the power of words of blessing. From the onset, she blessed Ruth. She spoke words of favor in her life. She wished her well. Her prayer for Ruth was not a lamentation before God but an intercession for her. She spoke words of faith in her life. The community spoke words of favor on Boaz and Ruth's marriage. In difficult times, we have to be mindful of what we say to ourselves and others.

14

They Were Joyful Amid Sadness

Happiness depends on happenings. It comes from the root word hap, which means "luck" or "circumstance." "I am happy today because things just happened to turn out right." Joy is different. It goes deeper. Joy is an attitude, a choice. Joy is an inside job and is not dependent on circumstances. It is your choice to rejoice.

—Rick Warren

First, Ruth enjoyed the kindness of Naomi when she agreed to travel with her. Since Ruth was determined to go with Naomi, you can imagine her joy when Naomi decided to travel with her. Naomi's act of kindness to journey with Ruth might have sent her over the moon. We can only imagine how this young widow was very excited to leave her home for Bethlehem in Judah. I believe with joy; she professed her faith in God and was ready to dare to dream.

Second, when Naomi and Ruth arrived in Bethlehem, they enjoyed the kindness of the custodians of Boaz's farm. Even without the approval of Boaz as the owner of the farm, the caretakers permitted Ruth to help herself in the farm. She didn't sow a seed, but she enjoyed the fruits of the seed sown by others because of the favor and hospitality of the custodians.

Third, Ruth enjoyed the kindness of Boaz. When Boaz came to his farm and saw Ruth, he asked his caretakers who she was. They told him the maiden from Moab who came with Naomi. Boaz didn't reverse the decision of his caretakers. He went further to give her more than Ruth had asked for. He offered her bread and wine and protection against possible harassment. If this didn't bring joy to Ruth, then nothing would. Ruth was even surprised by the kindness she received from Boaz, and she said, "Why have I found favor in your eyes, that you should take notice of me, when I am a foreigner?" (Ruth 2:10). Boaz replied that it was due to Ruth's kindness to Naomi. In effect, Ruth reaped the seed of goodness she showed to Naomi.

Fourth, Naomi enjoyed the generosity of Ruth when she brought food home. Ruth went to harvest not only for herself but also for Naomi. Imagine the joy of Naomi that there was enough food home for the two of them. Naomi was certainly glad for the generosity of Boaz. She said a prayer of blessing for Boaz for allowing them to enjoy the fruits of his farm.

Fifth, Naomi and Ruth arrived at the time of harvest. There is a joy when you find yourself in the right place and the right time. It was a time of grace and opportunity for Naomi and Ruth. You can picture the joy of these two women for the perfect timing. Nothing could have made them more joyful than coming at the time of abundance of food. If they had arrived at the time of hunger, that would have been a big misfortune for them, but they came at the right time.

Sixth, the elders and community rejoiced with Ruth and Boaz at their marriage. Marriage is usually a joyful event for the bride, groom, immediate family, and the community as a whole. In the case of Boaz and Ruth, the elders and the community expressed their joy in their solemn prayer of blessings for them. We can visualize the immense pleasure of Ruth on the day of her marriage after all that she went through.

Seventh, there was a joy for the birth of Obed. I am very sure that Naomi, Ruth, and Boaz rejoiced at the birth of Obed. We can't imagine the pleasure of Ruth becoming a mother. With joy, Naomi helped Ruth to nurse her baby boy as most grandmothers do. Naomi's dream came true; she became a granny. The community was filled with joy for Naomi, Ruth, and Boaz for the life of Obed.

The Lessons

1. Naomi and Ruth teach us that we can find joy, even in sadness. We may be unhappy about what happens to us without losing our joy. As we have seen, Naomi was an unhappy woman. To show her unhappiness, she changed her name Naomi, pleasantness, to Mara, bitterness. However, she had joy amid the sadness. She lost the company of her husband and two children, yet she found comfort in the company of Ruth.

2. How can you find joy amid sadness like Naomi and Ruth? How do you find solace amid sorrow like Naomi and Ruth? First, I suggest you believe and trust God. I ask you to pray and trust that God has a master plan even if you don't see it. I ask you to pray for your departed souls. It is not for us to judge those gone before us but to pray that God will be merciful to them. It is the right thing to do and ask God to decide their fate based on His mercy and not any merits.

Second, I invite you to learn the difference between happiness and joy. You may never be happy anytime, you remember the death of someone you loved, but you can rejoice for the good memories. You may not recover the loss of wealth but can rejoice for your life. The difference between happiness and joy is not academic or semantic. It is real, and it helps to know the difference and live what you have learned.

    i.   Happiness is based on facts and figures. Depending on the circumstances in question, you may be happy or unhappy. For instance, the loss of a loved one like a wife, husband, son, mother, brother, wealth, and job will make you unhappy. To be happy under such circumstances will be insane if not sociopathic. When bad things happen, we are unhappy, and there is nothing wrong with that. It shows our humanity.

ii. Figures make us happy or unhappy. Sometimes, higher numbers make us satisfied, and lower numbers make us miserable. For instance, politicians are happy with their high approval rate; priests and pastors are delighted with good church attendance. TV producers are so glad when their shows have a high approval rate. Happiness is about the increase and decrease of what happens to us. Studies show that some peoples' happiness, loneliness, self-esteem are significantly affected by the amount of time they spend on social media. The number of electronic thumbs up, likes on their Instagram or Facebook posts and pictures, contribute to the emotion they experience.[31]

iii. Happiness is big business. Intellectuals are significant participants in the happiness industry. A search on amazon.com on May 2, 2020, titled "happiness book" brought out over seventy thousand results. On the other hand, a search on the same day and a few minutes for "joy book" indicated twenty thousand. A similar search conducted on March 31, 2020, revealed sixty thousand results for "happiness book" on amazon.com and "joy book" twenty thousand results.

iv. A parallel search from google.com on May 2, 2020, titled "how to be happy" saw 7,940,000,000 results in (0.44 seconds) and "how to be joyful" revealed about 154,000,000 results in (0.41 seconds). A previous Google search on March 31, 2020, on "how to be happy" saw about 7,920,000,000 results in

---

[31] Melissa G. Hunt, Rachel Marx, Courtney Lipson, and Jordyn Young. *Journal of Social and Clinical Psychology*, Vol. 37, No. 10, 2018, pp. 751–768, *Trevor Haynes*, http://sitn.hms.harvard.edu/flash/2018/dopamine-smartphones-battle-time/ retrieved May 1, 2020

(0.50 seconds) and "how to be joyful" 121,000,000 results in (0.50 seconds). The numbers from both tech giants about happiness and joy are *res ipsa loquitur*—i.e., the facts speak for themselves.

v. Joy is God's gift to His sons and daughters. In the New Testament, joy is one of the spiritual gifts. It is a gift of the Holy Spirit. Joy is a recognition that I am a child of God. It recognizes that I came to this world not by chance but by God's choice and plan. You can't teach people to be joyful, but you can teach people to be happy. You can only help people to discover the joy that is within them. Joy is a discovery of God's unconditional love for us.

vi. For Christians, our joy is based on what Jesus did for us on Calvary. According to C. S. Lewis, "The Christian is in a different position from other people who are trying to be good. They hope, by being good, to please God if there is one, or—if they think there is not—at least they hope to deserve approval from good men. But the Christian thinks any good he does come from the Christ-life inside him. He does not think God will love us because we are good, but that God will make us good because He loves us; just as the roof of a greenhouse does not attract the sun because it is bright, but becomes bright because the sun shines on it" (C. S. Lewis, *Mere Christianity*).

vii. Happiness is a human pursuit, but joy is God's providential gift. Happiness is what you do for yourself or what others do for you, but joy is a gift. Like any gift, it has to be accepted or rejected. Happiness makes you comfortable, but joy makes you courageous. That is why Ruth was brave to leave home to a foreign land. Happiness is about feeling, and joy is about being. Joy thrives on who you are and happiness on how you feel. Happiness is external but joy is internal.

15

Ruth Made a Personal Choice of Faith

Real growth stops when you lose the tension between where you are and where you want to be. Ruth's story challenges us to lean into the tension. Ruth, having lost so much with the death of her husband, did not settle for heartache and pain.

—Michelle McClain-Walters, 2

And when Na'omi saw that she was determined to go with her, she said no more.

—Ruth 1:18

If Naomi and Ruth had a debate, Ruth won the debate. Thank God it was a conversation. Therefore, there was no winner or loser. Ruth's love just won the heart of Naomi. The decision made by Naomi to travel to her homeland with Ruth was in recognition of Ruth's determination. I believe Ruth convinced Naomi not because she presented superior arguments, facts, data, and information; it was not so much her possession of special communication skills and display of exceptional knowledge. Therefore, the question worth pondering is, "Why did Ruth's determination win Naomi's heart, or why was Ruth so determined to journey with Naomi?" We find the answer in the two preceding verses 16 and 17. These two verses give the reasons why Ruth was determined to journey with Naomi. The core of Ruth's determination to travel with Naomi was her desire to have three relationships.

First, Ruth wanted to continue her relationship with Naomi, albeit in a different way. Ruth stated that, "Where you go, I will go, where you lodge, I will lodge" (Ruth 1:16). She wanted to be in the company of Naomi. She was prepared to go and stop where Naomi will go and stop. It was more than a pledge of loyalty. It was a promise of a special relationship between two women who had experienced similar challenges and were ready to find a solution. Ruth wanted Naomi to lead her in search of a solution.

Second, Ruth was determined to connect with different people in a new community. She wanted to relate with Naomi's people when she stated, "Your people shall be my people" (Ruth 1:16). Here, Ruth manifested her belief in the importance of community. She believed that life was not just about the two of them but other people as well.

Third, Ruth intended to have a personal relationship with God. She said to Naomi, "Your God my God" (Ruth 1:16). That was Ruth's profession of faith in God.

Fourth, Ruth desired a lasting relationship with Naomi. Ruth was not seeking a relationship of convenience but an enduring one. She said to Naomi, "Where you die, I will die, and there will I be buried" (Ruth 1:17). Ruth was a realist, and she knew that she and Naomi would die one day, but before their death, they needed to support each other in a lasting relationship.

Fifth, Ruth's determination was anchored on prayer. She saw prayer as an expression of a personal bond with God. Ruth recognized that prayer was a physical connection with God known to all people by different names but had revealed Himself in a unique way to Israel as Yahweh. Ruth knew that human relationship with Naomi was time bound but her relationship with God was eternal. Therefore, she prayed to God. She asked for God's blessing in life and death. Ruth said, "May the Lord do so to me and more also if even death parts me from you" (Ruth 1:16). Ruth believed that even in death, God could bless her.

The above were the five reasons why Ruth was so determined to travel with Naomi. Ruth's determination was rooted in wisdom more than a hasty desire to leave home because of personal tragedies. She convinced Naomi because her choice to travel was informed by her faith in a personal God and not her information about the faith. Her decision was made out of conviction and not convenience. I believe that is why Naomi was convinced that it was right for Ruth to travel with her.

The Lessons

1. The need for "the other." Who is the other for you? For Ruth, the other was Naomi. Maybe for you, the other is your wife or husband, son or daughter, brother or sister, and a friend. We all need the other person to journey with us, especially in times of grief. We realize our need for others in a moment of crisis, such as the coronavirus pandemic. During the peak of COVID-19, we realized our dependence on one another, especially on health-care professionals and other essential service providers. In post-COVID-19, we need others to help us grieve and grow better than we were.

2. The need for community. Ruth recognized that life was not just about her and Naomi. She was aware that they were traveling to live in a community. Therefore, she was prepared to be part of her new community. We need our small communities; we need our country as a national community; we need other countries to create a better international community. As comity of nations, we can support one another to overcome our losses and build a stronger world economy that works for the poor and the rich. The adage, no man is an island, is more relevant for all of us today than ever before.

3. We need God. To overcome or deal with the pain of loss, we need God. Some people say, "We don't need God at all. We can take care of ourselves." Some people don't consider God as an

essential part of their life due to many reasons such as scandals from men of God—priests, prophets, pastors, bishops, evangelists, natural and personal tragedies, and their own upbringing.

Actually, some people don't have a problem with God but rather with the failures and hypocrisy of those who represent Him. They can't believe when God appears to be unconcerned when His Name is abused and exploited. For such people, it appears God is an accomplice of the evil committed in His Name. For others, their problem is God not giving them what they think they deserve or are entitled to receive. Therefore, they are just angry with God. They are just not on good terms with God. Some people's problem is that their minds cannot conceive God. God would be God if their minds and senses can perceive and program this awe and omniscience Being. For some people, the idea of total surrender to the invisible God who is the Creator and Caretaker of the world makes them feel too small and weak. Some people have a problem imagining the loving and all-good God amid all the darkness and evil in the world.

I am not sure whether any intellectual and scientific evidence of God's existence and goodness propounded by Thomas Aquinas and other great minds would do any good for unbelievers. It suffices to paraphrase Thomas Aquinas, "to the one who has faith, no explanation is necessary, but to one without faith, no explanation is possible."[32] Ruth made her profession of faith in the darkest moment of her life and never regretted it. She is an example of faith.

4. We need selfless love. We have to go beyond the "What is in it for me?" attitude. There is nothing wrong with taking care of ourselves, but we also need to help others. Ruth effectively teaches us that there is a blessing in giving than in receiving. Ruth validates the doctrine that it is in giving that we receive. Boaz recognized Ruth's selfless love and sacrifice when he said to her, "All that you have done for your mother-in-law since

---

[32] Summa Theologiae II-II, Q. 1, Art. 5, reply obj. 1)

the death of your husband has been fully told me, and how you left your father and mother and your native land and came to a people that you did not know before" (Ruth 2:11). The lesson is: when you do an act of kindness to those in need today, you have sown a seed of goodness for tomorrow.

5. We need to accept the reality of death and eternity. Both Ruth and Naomi accepted the pain of the deaths of their family members. They acknowledged their frustrations and loss. The two women did not belittle or magnify their pain. Ruth admitted that death was a reality. The good news is that there is also eternity after death. As a preacher once said, "for unbelievers, we live to die, but for believers, we die but to inherit eternal life." Sadly, we have to admit the reality of our death and that of our loved ones. However, faith in eternal life is a source of consolation amid the sorrow of death.

6. We need a journey. We need three types of journeys in time of loss. One is a physical journey, the second is a psychological journey, and the third is a spiritual journey. The physical journey requires resources and risks. If you can afford a reasonable risk, it is worth taking a vacation. Traveling to places you have always dreamt of visiting helps to reduce our sorrow of loss. A visit to good friends and relatives is a useful remedy to the pain of loss. If necessary and applicable, we can learn from Naomi and Ruth's physical journey to Judah.

The psychological journey is about mindfulness or meditation. It is staying calm and still. It is using the human mind to imagine the best, to meditate on where you were and where you are now. Just think about the millions of sperms and eggs out of which you became a seed in your mother's womb—an embryo. Imagine the choice for life by your mother. Such recognition helps to visualize the baby you were born and the man or woman you are today. It helps to ponder on the existential question, "Who am I?" The journey of traveling back in time helps to live the present in a meaningful way.

For some people, the spiritual journey begins with a profession of personal faith like Ruth. For others, it is a renewal of faith that was given at childhood but neglected and unnurtured. For some other people, their spiritual journey is an uninterrupted or continuous journey of faith in good and bad times. In a time of crisis, their faith is their greatest weapon. Whatever your circumstance, you need to take a personal journey of faith seriously.

16

Ruth Worked Hard

Ruth blasted through these barriers and became a lead-
ing woman in her newly adopted culture, a wife and
mother, an owner of the field she once gleaned, and one
of the few women named in the lineage of Christ.

—Michelle McClain-Walters, 11

Naomi and Ruth arrived in Bethlehem "at the beginning of barley
harvest" (Ruth 1:22). It was a good time for them because they were
two widows who journeyed from afar and arrived at harvesting time.
At their arrival in Bethlehem, Ruth said to Naomi, "Let me go to
the field, and glean among the ears of grain after him in whose sight
I shall find favor" (Ruth 2:2). Ruth went to work on Boaz's farm.
She didn't go with a begging bowl to fill her plates, but she did work
"from early morning without resting even for a moment" (Ruth 2:7).
Ruth worked so hard until the end of the barley and wheat harvest.
Her hard work might have caught the attention of Boaz who later
became her husband.

The Lessons

1. Ruth didn't just dream about a better future, but she worked
    hard for it. She left her country in search of a better life. When

Ruth finally arrived, she worked from dawn to dusk. She worked in a very difficult environment. Boaz had to guarantee her safety from being molested by young men on the farm. Ruth is an example of everyday hardworking women who risk their lives to feed their families. Boaz is an example of men who are concerned and care for the safety of women at the workplace.

2.   Ruth didn't just pray and wait for manna from heaven. As a woman of faith, I am sure Ruth prayed for her daily bread, but she also plied the land for the daily bread she prayed for. She teaches us the need to sweat to enjoy the sweetness of our labor. The lesson is that the answer to our prayer against famine is farming.

3.   Ruth teaches us the dignity of work. Ruth gives us an example that working at a farm is a dignified vocation. It feeds people. It provides food, which is our basic human need. During the peak of COVID-19, the world realized more than ever before the importance of farmers and those in the food supply business. We couldn't have survived without our hardworking farmers. In post-COVID-19, we need to appreciate and compensate our hardworking farmers. We need to have young men and women being proud before television cameras that they are farmers just like any highly rated profession.

17

Ruth Was Transparent and Accountable

There is an epidemic of individualism in our culture today that causes us to be so self-centered that we no longer seek to maintain fruitful, long-term relationships with others. But in this season those who receive favor and prosper will be those Ruths who remain loyal and committed to the people God has placed in their lives.

—Michelle McClain-Walters, 7

Ruth was a transparent person. She showed transparency by accounting to Naomi the things that came her way. Ruth reported to Naomi her encounters with Boaz. When Naomi needed more information, she answered Naomi's questions with honesty. Naomi also offered Ruth her sincere suggestions and wise counseling whenever Ruth opened up for help. They were honest with each other. They had a responsible and accountable relationship.

First, Ruth accounted for her labor. When Ruth went to Boaz's farm to harvest, she did so in complete transparency with Naomi. She was not only transparent but also shared the fruit of her labor with Naomi. Ruth offered Naomi, "What she had gleaned, and she also brought out and gave her what food she had left over after being satisfied" (Ruth 2:18). When Ruth shared her harvesting produce with Naomi, she showed self-accountability. She was not required by law but by love to freely be a good steward. Ruth understood the doctrine of giving back what she freely received from Boaz.

Second, Ruth answered Naomi's questions. When Naomi asked her, "Where did you glean today? And where have you worked?" (Ruth 2:19), Ruth did not see that as an invasion of her private life, but she told Naomi everything. She might have understood Naomi's inquiry as an occasion for conversation. I believe she shared her experience on the farm with enthusiasm with Naomi. We can imagine the sincere curiosity of Naomi to know more about how the day went for Ruth. I can picture the two of them gazing at each other and Naomi nodding to Ruth to tell her more about what happened on the farm. What an incredible experience they probably shared.

Third, Ruth shared with Naomi her encounter with Boaz. We can only imagine the excitement of Ruth narrating her experience with Boaz to Naomi. Boaz's kindness even surprised Ruth, so you can bet she shared the story with Naomi. Naomi was not just interested in the food Ruth was bringing home; she genuinely cared for the welfare of Ruth. Because of her concern, Naomi asked Ruth, "How did you fare, my daughter?" (Ruth 3:16). Ruth was so honest with Naomi, and she told her, "All that the man had done for her" (Ibid), and accounted for the gifts she received from Boaz.

The Lessons

1. We need transparency and accountability in our homes. Transparency requires sharing right or accurate information. It is an essential value in everyday life but indispensable in seeking solace for our loss. For example, if a bereaved person is seeking a professional help from a therapist, priest, teacher, lawyer, counselor, and doctor, she needs to be very transparent with the expert. Without transparency, it would be impossible to offer professional help. Accountability is equally necessary for professionals in dealing with their clients. It is required from both the client and the service provider.

2. We need transparency and accountability from public officials. Ruth's transparent character is an example for government officials. Elected and nonelected public officers need to learn from Ruth to be accountable to those they serve. Public figures who are not necessarily government officials may learn from Ruth's honesty and transparency. COVID-19 has taught us how the virtues of transparency and accountability are necessary for public health. In the wake of the pandemic, inaccurate information, absurd conspiracies, and false claims of a cure for COVID-19 didn't help.

3. We need accountability and transparency in international relations. Naomi and Ruth had a respectful, accountable, responsible, and honest relationship as two women from two different cultures—Ruth was from present-day Jordan, and Naomi from Israel. They are an excellent example of international relations among the comity of nations. There is an ongoing media debate in the global public square about how many facts the World Health Organization (WHO) should have known from China, and informed the world. What is undebatable is that accountability and transparency are essential for health in a globalized world. COVID-19 has taught us how sharing necessary health information is essential for saving lives. Transparency and accountability are essential virtues in rebuilding families, communities, and nations.

4. We need an accountable media. Ruth's sharing of micro-factual information with Naomi is an example for the way mass dissemination of information should work. The principle of accountability and transparency is necessary for both micro and macro information sharing. Traditional media should be held accountable, just as they hold everyone else accountable. Information about people's health, loss, and grief are sacred. Therefore, the sharing of such information, if necessary, requires faithful allegiance to facts and respect for families. Social media is a useful and powerful tool that has connected people worldwide, but there is a need for accountability by users and those who created the platform. The spread of misinformation, hatred, fear, and blatant disregard for the loss of others on social media platforms undermine our common humanity and basic human decency.

18

Naomi Mentored Ruth

Mentors will speak faith to you when you are doubting. They see who you are. Initially they have more faith in you than you have in yourself, and you are able to lean on that when things get hard and confusing.

—Michelle McClain-Walters, 94

Mentoring is parenting an adult who is ready to learn from a more knowledgeable, experienced, and wise person. Mentoring requires unlearning bad habits and acquiring new behavior. A mentor is like a nonbiological or legal parent. A good mentor assists the mentee in discerning her vocation and pursuing it. There are good examples of mentors in the Bible. For example, Jethro, the father-in-law of Moses, mentored Moses. In Exodus 18, Jethro coached Moses to become an effective leader. Jethro helped Moses to set up an efficient conflict resolution mechanism for the people of Israel. In the New Testament of the Bible, Paul mentored Timothy to be a successful preacher of the Gospel. Naomi, like mentors in the Old and the New Testaments, mentored her daughter-in-law Ruth to navigate her way in Judah as a foreigner.

First, when Naomi and Ruth arrived in Bethlehem, Naomi coached Ruth about her safety. As a responsible mentor, Naomi helped Ruth to steer her way to the safe corners of her new home.

Naomi said to Ruth, "It is well, my daughter, that you go out with his maidens, lest in another field, you be molested" (Ruth 2:22). Boaz had already directed her to a secured place of harvest, given that Ruth had no prior experience of the territory. Naomi, as the mentor of Ruth, reinforced Boaz's safety guidelines. A mentor counsels the mentee, and that is what Naomi did for Ruth's security and safety. There is nothing more important for a mentor than protecting the life of a mentee, and Naomi didn't fail in doing her job as a mentor.

Second, Naomi advised Ruth to dress up to meet Boaz. Naomi said to Ruth, "Wash, therefore and anoint yourself, and put on your best clothes and go down to the threshing floor" (Ruth 3:3). With her experience, Naomi knew the importance of physical appearance to a man. Given that Boaz was Naomi's kinsman, she probably knew the kind of impression that Ruth could make on him by providing such a thorough preparation. Naomi gave Ruth four instructions: to wash, anoint herself, wear the best clothes, and go down to the threshing floor. All the four instructions were necessary for Ruth going to meet her potential husband in a foreign country. The first time Boaz met Ruth was on a farm. Probably, he met Ruth in her farm clothes— dirty, worn out, and soaked with sweat. It is highly likely that Naomi wanted her to make the best impression this time with Boaz.

Third, Naomi advised Ruth about the importance of timing. Naomi instructed Ruth to wait for the right time or the perfect moment to make a good and lasting impression on Boaz. Naomi told Ruth, "But do not make yourself known to the man until he has finished eating and drinking. But when he lies down, observe the place where he lies; then, go and uncover his feet and lie down; and he will tell you what to do" (Ruth 3:4). She told Ruth to wait for Boaz to eat, drink, and lie down before any move. As an experienced woman, Naomi probably knew that a hungry man is often an angry man who would not have time for anyone. Naomi knew that beyond the physical appearance, Ruth had to know the right time to strike, to make a move, and to come on stage. Therefore, having told Ruth how to appear before Boaz, she also coached her on when to appear.

Naomi meticulously coached Ruth to meet Boaz. As to whether Naomi prepared Ruth for levirate marriage in the strict sense of the law in Deuteronomy or redemption in the book of Leviticus is a subject of scholarly debate amid diverse views.[33] What is indisputable is that Naomi played a significant role in Ruth's marriage with Boaz.

Ruth did exactly what she was told to do by Naomi. Ruth told Naomi all "that you say I will do" (Ruth 3:5), and she did. Ruth made herself coachable by obeying the instructions and the directions of Naomi. Her obedience paid off. There is no mentorship if the mentee is not disposed to learn. As a good mentee, Ruth met the love of her life by learning from Naomi, a wise and experienced woman.

The Lessons

1.   Some people fail to achieve their dreams not because they have a low IQ or they are less intelligent but because they don't obey instructions. Ruth gives us an example of the importance of trustful obedience. She had faith in Naomi's wisdom and experience. Therefore, she listened and learned from her. Ruth teaches us the lesson of trust and obedience to those in authority.

It is an undeniable fact that some people in a position of power and influence have abused their power. That makes some people suspicious and question those in a position of power like parents, teachers, priests, pastors, professors, politicians, directors, and managers. That, notwithstanding, there are good mentors with power and authority who genuinely help their mentees. One of the reasons we learn from mentors is that they may have made their own mistakes and are ready to share them for today's generation to avoid repeating the same mistakes.

2.   Naomi did not abuse her power and authority. Every suggestion, recommendation, instruction, and direction were for the interest of Ruth. That is what a good coach does. Naomi offers the world an example of parenting, coaching, counseling, and mentoring. Without honesty to help mentees, mentorship will

---

[33] Dvora E. Weisberg, *Levirate Marriage*, n.p. [cited 10 Jul 2020]. Online: https://www.bibleodyssey.org:443/people/related-articles/levirate-marriage

cease to exist. The world needs more mentors in the family, small communities, and our global village. We need mentors to help the new generation to navigate rough waters. Post-COVID-19 generation needs honest, responsible, and accountable mentors to help them navigate through the devastation of the coronavirus pandemic. As the world grieves the loss of life and properties, we need good mentors, experts, coaches, and advisers to help us go through our loss and quick recovery.

19

Boaz Intervened

Boaz "is indeed a man of true substance, marked by duty, grace, patience, and covenant loyalty."

—Sinclair B. Ferguson, 72

There are three significant Boaz's interventions in the lives of Naomi and Ruth that changed their lives forever. First, Boaz was generous to Ruth and Naomi. He provided them food from his farm. Second, he intervened as an administrator of Elimelech's estate. Third, Boaz married Ruth and began a new family. In all the three interventions, Boaz acted as an honorable man with dignity, self-respect, respect for Ruth, his kinsman, and the customs of his people.

a. Boaz and Ruth

Boaz recognized the worth of Ruth. He didn't see Ruth as a desperate woman for him to take advantage of her. He said, "All my fellow townsmen know that you are a woman of worth" (Ruth 3:11). Boaz admitted that he wasn't the only person who saw the value of Ruth; other men in Bethlehem did as well. Boaz met Ruth for the first time begging for food from his farm. With Naomi's help, Ruth went to Boaz's house, asking him to marry her effectively. Boaz responded with dignity and respect. Boaz didn't see Ruth as a beggar but his possible better self. He didn't see a poor anxious foreign widow but a God-fearing woman.

Boaz was honest with Ruth. He told Ruth that he was not the immediate kinsman. Boaz said to Ruth, "It is true that I am a near kinsman, yet there is a kinsman nearer than I" (Ruth 3:12). He urged her to be patient and wait for the necessary customary practices. Boaz admitted that his future with Ruth was contingent on his kinsman's decision. He, therefore, laid out his plans for her with clarity and dignity. Boaz didn't just talk but acted upon his words. He fulfilled his promise to Ruth when he woke up early morning and went to meet his kinsman.

b.   Boaz and His Kinsman

Boaz's first agenda of the day after meeting Ruth was to look for his kinsman. He woke up early morning and "went up to the gate and sat down there; and behold, the next of kin, of whom Bo'az had spoken, came by. So Bo'az said, 'Turn aside, friend; sit down here'; and he turned aside and sat down" (Ruth 4:1). Boaz told his kinsman to make his choice. The first choice is to redeem the land of Elimelech. The second choice was consequential to the first choice, which was to redeem Ruth, Naomi, and honor Elimelech with a child.

With clarity, Boaz told his kinsman, "'If you will redeem it, redeem it; but if you will not, tell me, that I may know, for there is no one besides you to redeem it, and I come after you.' And he said, 'I will redeem it.' Then Bo'az said, 'The day you buy the field from the hand of Na'omi, you are also buying Ruth the Moabite, the widow of the dead, in order to restore the name of the dead to his inheritance.' Then the next of kin said, 'I cannot redeem it for myself, lest I impair my own inheritance. Take my right of redemption yourself, for I cannot redeem it'" (Ruth 4:4–6). Boaz showed respect by prioritizing his kinsman. He didn't use his wealth and power to ignore his kinsman's right. That shows how honorable Boaz was. He didn't bully his kinsman but reasoned with him about his options.

c. Boaz and the Community

Boaz respected the laid-down rules and customs. He didn't ignore the tradition and public procedures because of his power and wealth. After calling his kinsman, he involved the community by stating his case in the presence of the "ten men of the elders of the city, and said, 'Sit down here'; so they sat down. Then he said to the next of kin, 'Na'omi, who has come back from the country of Moab, is selling the parcel of land which belonged to our kinsman Elim'elech. So I thought I would tell you of it, and say, Buy it in the presence of those sitting here, and in the presence of the elders of my people'" (Ruth 4:2–4). He made his community part of the process of redemption. He knew the protocols of his community, and he did respect them.

The Lessons

1. Boaz's respect for Ruth, his kinsman, and the custom of his people is exemplary. He teaches us how to treat others with respect. It is very easy to treat people above you with respect because of what they can do for you. It takes a person of honor to respect those below him. Boaz's respect for Ruth is an example for men of power and influence. Boaz treated Ruth who was a poor foreigner with dignity and touched on the core of his person. Boaz lived in a patriarchal society where men had enormous power over women, but he treated Ruth with respect at all times.

2. Despite all the progress the world has made, in some parts of the world, women are unfortunately commercialized, monetized as commodities for men's sexual pleasure and erotic satisfaction. In other parts of the world, girls and women are discriminated against and denied economic and political access. We have so much to learn from Boaz on how to treat women with respect.

3. Boaz's respect for his kinsman and the community's tradition is an equally important lesson for us today. Some men who have power and influence don't like to obey rules. They think rules are for others and not for them. They don't show respect to oth-

ers and reasonable time-tested procedures. They use their power and position to get anything and do anything they want. David, a grandson of Boaz, is an example of such men who used his power to plan the death of Uriah after his amorous relationship with his wife, Bathsheba, and married her (2 Samuel 11:1–26). There are such men like David today, that is why we need to learn from Boaz.

4. Boaz did not undermine the customs of his people. He teaches us respect for rules, norms, traditions, and customs necessary for the community's survival. He went through all the transactional procedures. As an honorable man, he did what was right. Boaz teaches us that rules, laws, procedures, customs, and norms are not always the imposition of the will of the powerful to oppress the poor. We learn from Boaz that rules are necessary to maintain stability, justice, and order in a community.

Boaz was charitable to Naomi and Ruth. He obeyed the rules but went beyond the rules. He gave food to Ruth and Naomi not because of any legal obligation but as a moral imperative to help two women in need of help. Boaz teaches us that a "society based solely on law is better-but perhaps only marginally better-than a society without it. In one the letter of the law might kill, if lawlessness kills in the other."[34] Respect for rules, procedures, and protocols are necessary, but they need humanity and charity. That is the lesson that we can learn from Boaz. For him, "law and love are one."[35]

---

[34] A. Sharma, *The Religious Perspective: Dignity as a Foundation for Human Rights Discourse*, in *Human Rights and Responsibilities in the World Religion*, Oxford 2003, 67–76.

[35] Sinclair B. Ferguson, 69.

20

Marriage, Family, and Generation

During her secret, nocturnal visit to the threshing floor
(ch. 3), Ruth proposed marriage to Boaz (3:9).

—Robert L. Hubbard, Jr., *The Book*
of Ruth, Michigan 1998, 51

The story of Ruth ends with the three institutions that are the heart of human civilization: marriage, family, and raising a new generation. First, there was a marriage between Boaz and Ruth. Second, there was a new family. Marriage creates couples, and a child in marriage creates a nuclear family. Therefore, "Boaz took Ruth, and she became his wife and he went in to her, and the Lord gave her conception, and she bore a son" (Ruth 4:13).

Third, Boaz, Ruth, Naomi, and the community welcomed a new baby. In fact, "the women of the neighborhood gave him a name, saying, 'A son has been born to Na'omi.' They named him Obed" (Ruth 4:17). Fourth, there was a new generation from the marriage of Boaz and Ruth. Obed, the son of Boaz and Ruth, became "the father of Jesse, the father of David. Now these are the descendants of Perez: Perez was the father of Hezron, Hezron of Ram, Ram of Ammin'adab, Ammin'adab of Nahshon, Nahshon of Salmon" (Ruth 4:17–20).

The Lessons

1. We may be tempted to think that Ruth and Naomi's story is an ancient narrative, therefore, of less importance to our complex society. We may take pride in ourselves for being more enlightened and progressive. But if you pause for a moment and imagine thousands of years ago, the poor people of Bethlehem accepted, celebrated, and embraced a marriage between a Moabite and Israelite. We realize that we have much to learn from them.

   A supposedly pre-Enlightenment and un-technological people did not outlaw intertribal marriage. However, a democratic, enlightened, learned, advanced, civilized, and a Christianized society prevented two consenting adults—a man and a woman—from marrying because of their geographical origin and the color of their skins (Loving v. Virginia, 388 U.S. 1, 1967). Imagine in 1958, the state of Virginia banned marriage between Mildred Loving, a black woman, and Richard Loving, a white man based on the Virginia Racial Integrity Act of 1924.

   Compare and contrast that with an ancient community of Bethlehem joyfully celebrated an intertribal marriage of a Moabite and Israelite. Shouldn't this humble us to learn? If we think we are more advanced and civilized than ancient cultures, let us remember the litigations that were fought, protests that were marched, the loss of lives, and the battles fought before people could do what Boaz and Ruth did thousands of years ago. They give us a lesson for a world filled with hatred to learn to love.

2. Boaz and Ruth's marriage was open to procreation. Boaz and Ruth opened their marriage to the possibility of God blessing them with a child. Thank God Obed came as a gift from God. The birth of Obed began a new generation, including David and Jesus Christ of Nazareth.

3. The mourning of Naomi and Ruth turned merry as Ruth married Boaz, and Ruth gave birth to Obed. Naomi and Ruth had

nothing, but with faith, God blessed them abundantly. Naomi and Ruth's losses were irreplaceable, but God gave them many reasons to rejoice again. Ruth became a wife and mother, and Naomi became a grandmother. They had their daily bread and had a roof over their heads. They eventually had all the essentials of life. Imagine the years when they had nothing and wailed for the loss of their husbands, yet they found a joyful new life with faith in God.

4. Ruth, the beggar, became the boss's wife. Imagine those custodians of Boaz's farm whom Ruth begged to harvest from the farm probably had to work for Ruth after her marriage with Boaz. Consider the maidens whom Boaz ordered Ruth to work with possibly had to work for their boss's wife, Ruth. All of them had to work for the woman who came to beg for food from them. The adage, "be nice to people on your way down because you might meet them on your way up," is so true.

5. Finally, may I reiterate that Naomi and Ruth's story teaches the fundamental difference between happiness and joy. Happiness is about events and things. Joy is about a relationship with God. Naomi's marriage to Elimelech was an event. That marriage was a bond to end with death. Naomi giving birth to two sons was probably the most significant event of her life. The passing away of them was the saddest event of her life. But she found joy. The darkness that hovered around Naomi and Ruth did not stay forever. The light of joy overcame the night of grief. The death of their husbands was horrible, but Ruth and Naomi did not allow the horror and the shock to hold them back from moving on.

They prayed to God and took practical actions. I wrote this book so that you may learn from the steps of Naomi and Ruth. I agree with Carolyn Custis James that for we, Christians, the story of Ruth is the story of God who accompanied all the characters in the book, especially Naomi, Ruth, and Boaz in their good and bad times. In the end, each actor in the book had to respond to God's presence and silence, but God was never absent in their lives. In the darkest night of your life, I urge you not to confuse God's silence with His absence.

Epilogue

Naomi and Ruth grieved by taking twenty steps that are enumerated below. I invite you to learn from their efforts in dealing with your loss.

1. *Admit your loss.*
    It is difficult to admit that your baby, husband, wife, sibling, friend, and hero is gone. Acknowledging the reality of your loss and all that comes with loss—pain, displeasure, anger, frustration, and desperation—is the beginning of the healing process.

2. *Grieve in your way.*
    Grieving is human, so accept your humanity. You may cry, sigh, and groan. People grieve differently. Some do it publicly, and others do it privately. There is no need to suppress your emotions. You have to learn to express them healthily.

3. *Ask questions.*
    Ask your therapist, priest, pastor, and rabbi questions. They may not have all the answers, but by asking, you give voice to your thoughts. You also get others to think. Don't be afraid to ask yourself and God tough questions, but patiently wait for the answers. When the answers do come, humbly accept them.

4. *Have a plan for the next stage of your life.*
    Loss can cripple you and crumble everything you have built. To overcome that, reengage yourself in a good cause. Don't rush into the next planning process. It would help to give it much

thought. You may seek a professional help to make significant decisions about the next stage of your life.

5. *Have a conversation.*
   Talk and listen to your family, friends, professionals, and genuinely interested people who are willing to listen to you. Be ready to listen to others, too, because that is the way to converse.

6. *Stay connected.*
   Sometimes it is good to be alone to enjoy silence but don't confuse silence with loneliness. The two are different things. Silence is being with yourself and listening to your voice and the voice of your Creator. Loneliness is the loss of yourself and missing your family, friends, and community. Loneliness is unhealthy, but silence is helpful. Avoid isolation and stay united and connected with good people.

7. *Seek change if necessary.*
   Be ready for reasonable changes. Dealing with loss requires some adjustment and adaptation. Sometimes change is uncomfortable and inconvenient, but it is the price we must pay for growth and maturity.

8. *Be sympathetic and empathetic.*
   Treat yourself well. Love yourself so that you can love others better. Don't overrate your pain, and don't underestimate the pain of others. Be kind to others, even amid your pain, and kindness will come back to you.

9. *Have faith.*
   Faith fortifies us to fight our fears and face the demon of despair. Open your eyes to see God in front of you, open your hearts for God to enter, open your mind for God to enlighten you, commend your spirit into God's hands, and surrender your soul to God. When you have done your part, leave God to take care of the rest.

10. *Celebrate life.*
    Mourning is a sad way of celebrating the life of the dead. Even in grief, we could still find time to celebrate the good memories of a loved one. I suggest that you find time to celebrate the living too before you lose them.

11. *Play by the two universal rules.*
    First, *do not do unto others what you do not want others to do to you.* Second, *do unto others what is right.* When you break these two rules, forgive yourself and forgive those who do not play by the rules that might have contributed to your loss. Please don't allow them to hurt you twice by holding on to hurt.

12. *Be patient with yourself and others.*
    Grieving is complicated. It is a very windy road; therefore, it requires a dose of patience every day. Some days you wake up doing great and feeling good, then you take a big sigh of relief. The next day you are feeling sad all over again. You have to be patient, endure, and persevere.

13. *Please pray.*
    Pray for yourself and the souls departed. Pray to see the beauty of life here on earth before you cross over to the other side of life. Pray for solace amid the sorrow, pray for serenity amid the sadness, pray for peace to overcome the pain of loss.

14. *Find joy.*
    We pursue happiness, but we discover joy. We need both joy and happiness because happiness prepares us for joy. Therefore, don't stop at happiness but dig deeper to find joy. Happiness is outside, but joy is within you. Joy is God's gift implanted in you to help you handle any setbacks. Joy straightens you up when you stumble.

15. *Dare to dream.*

    Almost everyone has a dream, but not everyone is determined to live their dreams. That is the difference between dreamers and dropouts—people who drop out may not believe in their dreams or do not pursue them. Take a leap of faith, trusting in God's goodness, and chase your dream.

16. *Work hard for a better life.*

    It is not enough to dream. You have to work hard for it. Stand up when you fall and continue the journey. Jesus fell many times on the road to Calvary, but he rose after every fall to finish the journey. Don't give up on yourself. Try again and again, and remember you are not alone in the journey. Jesus Christ is with you every step of the way.

17. *Be transparent and accountable.*

    Be honest to yourself, family, friends, and professionals, helping you recover from your loss. Self-accountability helps you to examine your actual state. Look at yourself in the mirror and ask, "Do I want to stay sad for the rest of my life?" Answer that question, sincerely. Does your loved one want you to be sad forever? Answer that question honestly.

18. *Help others for helping sake.*

    Reach out to help someone who needs your help. You can make a difference in the lives of others. Generosity for the sake of charity is satisfying. Helping those in need is a miracle. It transforms families and guarantees generations after generations a better life.

19. *Accept help.*

    As you help others, there are times we also need the help of others. It would be best if you were humble to ask for help and accept it when given. Accept professional services if need be. Always remember that getting help doesn't make you inferior and the giver superior. It just means they are caring for you and sharing God's blessings with you.

20. *Build a relationship.*

Try to build bridges and not walls. Please, don't separate yourself from others. You need your family, friends, and community. We were made for one another. Let nothing superficial separate you from our shared humanity. Please don't lie to yourself that you are self-made or you can do it alone. No human being is self-made or an island. The truth is that:

1
we are not here[36]
by chance
but by God's choice.

2
we are here,
not by desire
but by God's design.

3
we are here,
not by our efforts,
but by God's thought,

4
we came here,
from nothing to something,
from nobody to somebody,
from nowhere to somewhere.

---

[36] Thomas Oppong-Febiri, We, (Modified), in *Anthology of Truth-Faith-Hope and Love*, Accra, 2017.

5

not only by trying,
but by treading
on God's teaching,

6

we can make it,
from zero to heroes,
from losers to winners,
from sinners to saints,
from crawling to soaring,
from mourning to merry.

7

not only by growing,
but by God's grace,
we can make it,
from unity to uniqueness,
from running fast to far.

8

not only by our sights,
but by God on our side,
unity will not only strengthen us,
but will straighten our paths.

9

not only by our minds
but by God's mercy,
we will not only narrate history,
but we will make history.

About the Author

Thomas Oppong-Febiri, M.A., LL.M., J.C.D. is a Catholic priest of Sunyani Diocese in Ghana. He is currently an associate pastor at St. Matthew and Our Lady of Perpetual Help-OLPH Parish, Hastings-on-Hudson and Ardsley in the Archdiocese of New York.

CPSIA information can be obtained
at www.ICGtesting.com
Printed in the USA
BVHW031727110521
607040BV00007B/1131